Trappers and Traders of the Far West

Come, my tan-faced children,
Follow well in order, get your weapons ready;
Have you your pistols? have you your sharp edged axes?
Pioneers! O Pioneers!

Walt Whitman

TRAPPERS AND TRADERS OF THE FAR WEST

--- ★ ---

Written and Illustrated by

JAMES DAUGHERTY

Landmark BOOKS

RANDOM HOUSE · NEW YORK

Contents

PART THREE

The Return East

June 29, 1812—April 30, 1813

Foreword

THE IMMENSE SCENE OF THIS STORY OF THE Astorians' march is the vast area of America extending from the Mississippi River to the Pacific Ocean. For backbone and roof tree of this vast land, the Rocky Mountains rise to the great Continental Divide. Steeply its western slopes plunge to the Pacific. Eastward its watershed descends gently across the great plains to the Mississippi.

The Astorians advanced into this unknown region with an iron resolve to push on to the farthest horizon beyond which lay their distant goal. They were equipped with a native ingenuity with which they met and mastered the sudden hazards and perils which each day's wayfaring so unexpectedly brought forth.

Deviously they advanced across the great plains to find the sources of the Snake. This mysterious river they knew would take them to the Columbia. Although these wanderers were without maps or guides, they still could trust the rivers. The Missouri, the Snake, the Columbia and their tributaries were certain guides. Following them they knew that "somewhere the weariest river winds safely home to sea."

Through the bitter winter weather the half-starved band staggered on their hunger march down the dark canyons of the Snake to reach the Columbia and their final destination on the shores of the Pacific. These men had a genius for survival that saw them through.

The long chronicle of their straggling and incredible adventures (they never seemed really to get lost) makes an heroic saga of an unbeatable race. In it stirs the pulse beats of the onrushing spirit of America, saying, "The difficult we do now, the impossible takes a little longer."

Their wanderings across the unexplored regions of the continent and back make a vivid picture tapestry, filled with barbaric processionals, and fantastic figures in violent action and slow motion. The foreground is rich with sharp details of costume and trappings, with beasts and birds; the background majestic with vistas of wild and craggy distances.

Not less dramatic is the tragic voyage of the *Tonquin* in its storm-tossed passage across two oceans and around two continents; its Odyssey among tropic islands and along storm-racked coasts to sudden and complete disaster.

Strangest of all is that this world-embracing dream of free enterprise, with all this stupendous effort, should collapse in futility and defeat only to rise again as a rich twofold empire, two great nations dwelling side by side in everlasting and unbroken peace.

Such were the desperate beginnings and glorious finale of Mr. Astor's far-flung dream.

JAMES DAUGHERTY

PART
I
VOYAGE
of the
TONQUIN

TONQUIN

The Nineteenth Century
Puts On a New Hat

ALONG SOUTH STREET IN NEW YORK CITY THE jibs of square-rigged merchant ships overhung the busy street. Their tall masts and rigging made a spidery forest of ropes and spars against the sky. Stevedores swarmed over the docks and jostled in the street as they shifted cargoes. The pungent smell of hides, spices, coffee and strange foreign odors scented the fresh harbor breeze. In the grog shops of the waterfront, Yankee sailors sat and told strange tales made of lies, fancies, and, the naked truth strangest of all.

3

A tremendous energy throbbed in the streets and shipping offices. Trade was booming and swift Yankee packets plowed the seven seas of the world with fabulous cargoes under their hatches.

The young Republic was exuberant in the first flush and bloom of Liberty, and the sky was the limit. The Constitution itself was only twenty-one years old. Wise President James Madison, who had been one of its principal framers, sat in the new President's Mansion in Washington, carrying on the policies of his friend, democratic "long Tom" Jefferson.

On the high seas British warships were holding up American merchantmen and taking off sailors who, it was claimed, were British subjects.

Across the Allegheny Mountains, Democracy was spilling out of its cradle to raise tall corn, huge hogs, fabulous mules, and fast horses in the Ohio valley. Jefferson and Congress had declared the Northwest Territory forever free, and revolutionary generals and veterans were chasing Indians out of Indiana and Illinois. Daniel Boone and his stalwart sons had already crossed the Mississippi and were staking out fat lands in Missouri.

Westward the Missouri, the Big Muddy, wound

like a great snake out of endless prairies where the grass grew six feet high. Against the farthest horizon the fabulous Stony Mountains lifted their white peaks against the turquoise sky, and rumbled with a mystic thunder. Here in their secret fastnesses were the sources of the Missouri, and here the Beaver people lived in the stillness of a timeless peace.

Wisest and most harmless of all the children of the wilderness, they built their round lodges. With the know-how of skilled engineers they raised stout dams across the mountain streams. Blissfully they slapped the water with their broad tails, and the sharp reports broke the stillness of the wilderness night like rifle shots.

Against the terrific cold of the mountain winters, each beaver wore a coat of glistening fur which was thick and warm and wondrous soft. But it was this handsome jacket that invited the beavers' destruction. In twos and threes, trappers were pushing up wilderness rivers and streams to their secret sources, looking for "sign" of beaver. Traders were venturing ever farther among the savage tribes of the western plains, offering scalping knives and raw alcohol for beaver pelts.

History always wears a hat. It changes the style of its headgear and puts on a new top piece as it marches from one age to the next. The seventeenth century wore a tall peaked hat with a great flopping brim. The eighteenth century had fastened up this untidy brim into the neat three-cornered hat, or tricorne. Now the nineteenth century was stepping out with a high round cylinder atop its noggin. This strange headpiece was made of glistening beaver fur and so was called a beaver hat, a top hat, high hat, or stovepipe.

This new top piece stood for fashion, for prestige, importance and power. Men sized each other up by the state of their beaver hats and the angles at which they wore them on their noodles.

The demand for high hats in Europe and America was using up more beaver fur than the free trappers and the Indian traders could supply.

Mr. Astor's Plan

New York was becoming the business center of the fur trade in the United States and business was booming. In this city of smart traders John Jacob Astor was the smartest of all.

Born in Waldorf, Germany, on July 17, 1763, he had gone to London with his brother at the age of sixteen. There the two had established a business in the manufacture and sale of musical instruments.

In 1784 Astor arrived in New York with a fiddle under his arm and a burning ambition to gain success in the New World.

In the free air of the new Republic prosperous merchants were building fortunes. Twenty-year-old John Jacob Astor listened with keen interest to the tall talk of the Manhattan fur merchants. Before long he sold his stock of musical instruments and invested his small capital in furs. In London and in Montreal he learned more about the possibilities of this far-flung business. By his cleverness and industry he became in a few years one of America's richest merchants.

Mr. Astor's imagination was reaching boldly toward new fields of action. As the details of his plan became clear in his practical mind he decided that the time to act had come.

A number of gentlemen connected with the fur trade were invited to Mr. Astor's office on a certain day. The subject of the meeting, he said somewhat vaguely, was a matter of importance. When his guests arrived it appeared that most of them were British subjects—Scotsmen and Canadians who had been in the service of the Northwest Company. Before leaving Mr. Astor's office these men had agreed to take part in the most dazzling enterprise of which anyone, even in those booming times, had ever dreamed.

This was, in effect, a scheme to peel the hides off all the unfortunate fur-bearing animals in North America, a plan to control, eventually, the fur trade of the world. Mr. Astor was to be the director. He would provide the capital (some $400,-000) and control fifty per cent of the shares of the Company. His ten partners would control the other fifty per cent and carry out his directions, although this meant endangering their shirts, their skins, and their lives.

MR JOHN
JACOB
ASTOR

The Company would at once set about establishing a chain of trading posts extending from St. Louis up the Missouri, across the Rockies, and down the Columbia to the Pacific. Mr. Astor hoped, if possible, to ruin or absorb all competitors, particularly the British Northwest Company.

The fur markets of Europe and China would be supplied by the Company's ships, and trade would be established with the Russians in Alaska. Other parts of the globe could later be developed, but at present this plan would do for a modest start.

As Mr. Astor detailed his plan, his friends were at first somewhat goggle-eyed. Then, as they listened, they became pleasantly bedazzled, and finally signed up with enthusiasm.

A trading post at the mouth of the Columbia was to be the key of the whole plan. There was no time to lose. Mr. Astor pointed out that foreign trading ships were already operating on the Pacific Coast and the Northwest Company was moving rapidly westward across the Canadian wilderness.

To make doubly sure of success there would be two expeditions. One was to travel by land from Montreal to the Mississippi, up the Missouri, across the Stony Mountains and down the Columbia.

Another party would go to the Columbia by sea around the Horn. The overland trip was some four thousand miles, not as the crow flies, but as the rivers wind. The sea voyage was a mere twenty thousand miles or so around most of the Western Hemisphere.

The Tonquin
(September 6, 1810)

Mr. Astor lost no time in preparing for the expedition. He engaged the *Tonquin*, a stout ship of some two hundred and ninety tons burden, for the Pacific voyage.

In August, 1810, the *Tonquin* was taking on cargo at her berth in New York harbor. Firearms, ammunition, tools, Indian goods, provisions, clothing, and the frame of a small schooner to be assembled on the Pacific coast filled her hold and cluttered her decks. Astor had engaged as her captain a Lieutenant Jonathan Thorn, on leave from the

13

United States Navy. He was an excellent navigator and a man of strict discipline who had, it developed, a fatally ungovernable temper.

Besides the *Tonquin's* crew of twenty-two men, there were thirty-three passengers. Twelve were clerks, thirteen were French voyageurs, and three were mechanics. Four were partners in the Company—Duncan McDougal, Alexander McKay, David Stuart and his nephew Robert. Nine of the voyageurs had paddled and portaged a large birch-bark canoe from the St. Lawrence River to the Hudson River by way of Lake Champlain. They had come down the Hudson singing Canadian boat songs and had arrived on a Sunday off the New York waterfront. There they were received with cheers by the amazed citizens.

To add to the excitement it was rumored that a British frigate was waiting off the coast. Her captain would board the *Tonquin* and take off all British subjects.

As the *Tonquin* cleared the Narrows and put to sea a man-of-war came bearing down upon her. To Captain Thorn's great relief it proved to be the United States frigate *Constitution*, which escorted the *Tonquin* safely out of sight of land.

The first day at sea the Captain assigned quarters and laid down the ship's rules. The voyageurs liked neither the quarters nor the rules, and the passengers from the frontier made it clear they were not in the habit of being ordered about.

From among the four partners Mr. Astor had selected Mr. Duncan McDougal to act as his representative. When Captain Thorn ordered all lights out sharply at eight o'clock Mr. McDougal ignored the order. He considered it an insult to Mr. Astor and to the clan of McDougal. The furious Captain threatened to put the Scotsman in chains. McDougal, brandishing his pistol, dared the Captain to try it. The prospect of a pleasant voyage seemed dim from the start.

To the Captain's disgust the Canadian boatmen soon became seasick and messed up their quarters. As the voyage wore on the Captain developed an ungovernable dislike for the voyageurs. Their untidy habits, their aversion to soap, and their French boat songs gave him tantrums.

Violent arguments took place between the terrible-tempered Captain and the four partners over who should give and who should take orders. Navy discipline and the easy-going ways of backwoods-men did not mix on the decks of the *Tonquin*. Soon the passengers and crew were not on speaking terms.

Day by day the *Tonquin* plowed southward through the heaving blue-black seas of the mid-Atlantic. As she came into the equatorial latitudes terrible storms lashed her with mountains of gray-green sea. Under the equatorial sun, the passengers broiled and thirsted on the blistering decks. After weeks of seafaring they sighted the black rocks of the Falkland Islands and put in for a supply of fresh water.

While the crew and Canadians were filling the water casks, the four partners and five clerks went ashore in a small boat. The delighted backwoods-men wandered over the islands hunting the sea birds, ducks, geese, and penguins that inhabited the barren rocks. The partners had clambered to the remotest parts of the islands in pursuit of the un-happy penguins.

Suddenly the men heard wild yells and someone shouting, "The ship's off!" Rushing back to the boat, they saw the *Tonquin* putting out to sea under full sail. They had failed to hear the ship's signal for departure.

The nine abandoned men put to sea in their small boat and rowed furiously in pursuit. The sea was rough, night was coming on, and the *Tonquin* was fast disappearing. Their situation was growing more desperate every moment.

On the *Tonquin*, young Mr. Robert Stuart, whose Uncle David had gone ashore, realized with horror that Captain Thorn had no intention of putting back to pick up the boat. Mr. Stuart seized his pistols and rushed to the Captain. "Order the ship about and pick them up or you are a dead man this instant," the young man shouted.

The *Tonquin* put about. In spite of the darkness and the wild sea, the boat crew finally reached the decks of the *Tonquin*. Captain Thorn said he had only put back because the wind had changed. Hatred flared up anew against the Captain. Crew and passengers kept to themselves, glaring at each other without speaking.

It was nearly four months after they left New York, nine thousand miles astern, that the *Tonquin* rounded the Horn and sailed out on the long swells of the Pacific. Weeks later the ship's lookout sighted the blue peak of Mona Loah on Owhyee, one of the Sandwich Islands. Along the rail of the

Tonquin the ship's crew stood eagerly eyeing the island paradise.

There came a sharp cry, "Man overboard!"

The sudden yell startled the ship's crew into action. A boy had fallen out of the forward rigging into the sea. Barrels, hen coops, benches, anything that would float was thrown overboard to save him. Meanwhile a small boat had been dropped overside to pick him up. By the time the boy was pulled into the rescue boat he was apparently drowned.

When the boat reached the *Tonquin*, the Captain would not permit the rescuers to board the ship with the boy. Instead he ordered them to pick up the junk that had been thrown overside. It was half an hour before they could return to the ship and try to revive the boy. After vigorous rubbing and rolling he began to breathe, his eyes opened, and life returned.

The Sandwich Islands
(February 11-28, 1811)

After bleak months on the heaving decks of the *Tonquin* it was good to feel solid earth under foot. On shore leave the passengers and crew wandered over the enchanted island. With awe they stood amid the bullet-scarred tree trunks where Captain Cook had been murdered in 1779.

While the ship took on water Captain Thorn dickered with the shrewd King of the islands for a supply of pork. The passengers and crew continued to explore the island paradise. The voyageurs sang their French boat songs and danced for the laughing natives. In turn, the voyageurs were feasted by the golden-skinned Polynesians who sang and danced to South Sea rhythms.

Finding the natives good companions, the Canadians invited forty Owyhees to join the ship's crew for the rest of the voyage. However, the Captain said there was room for only twenty-four. Meanwhile the partners inquired into the possibilities of the islands as a post in the China trade.

After eleven days the *Tonquin* was ready to set sail on the last leg of her long voyage. Because the ship's boat and some of her crew were delayed by heavy weather, the impatient Captain put off without her. For six hours the abandoned sailors rowed through a wild sea trying to overtake the ship. Finally the Captain ordered the *Tonquin* put about and picked up the boat.

By this time the Captain's frenzies and rages had settled into an obsession. He fancied the passengers were plotting to murder him. The Canadians now would speak only in French, and the Scotsmen used the Gaelic language, neither of which the Captain understood. He became more suspicious as he saw the clerks scribbling in their journals. He suspected that the words they wrote were not paying him any compliments. A dark spirit of foreboding settled upon the ill-fated ship as she drove north through stormy seas.

The Mouth of the Columbia
(Landfall March 22, 1811)

It was a wild March day when the storm-tossed *Tonquin* sighted the coast of Oregon. Four miles to the north the headland of Cape Disappointment rose grayly. White surf stretched across the bay where the heavy Pacific breakers roared on sandy bars that obstructed the entrance.

Somewhere among these breakers Captain Thorn must find a channel deep enough to take the *Tonquin* into the bay. It was a perilous passage for even so expert a navigator as Thorn.

The Captain called sharply to the first mate. "Mr. Fox, you will proceed in the ship's boat with five men and find a channel of four fathoms." He named a sailor, an old Frenchman, and three boys who were not sailors to man the boat.

"I must have seamen to handle a boat in such a sea, sir," said the mate.

"Mr. Fox, if you are afraid of salt water you should have remained at Boston," said Thorn angrily.

Mr. Fox had always been friendly with the passengers and so had earned the Captain's hatred. The Astor partners pleaded with Thorn to wait until the weather grew calmer but this only served to make him more angry.

"My uncle was drowned here not many years ago, and now I am going to lay my bones with his," Fox said as he shook hands with his friends and shoved off in the leaky boat.

From the deck the passengers could see the boat rise and disappear in the heavy seas. She became a black speck against the wall of white surf and was finally lost to sight. To the passengers it seemed that they had seen five men sent to death in cold blood.

22

PACIFIC OCE[AN]

SANDWICH
ISLANDS

THE
VOYAGE
of the
TONQUIN

The next day another boat from the ship made several unsuccessful attempts to find the channel. The following morning the Captain ordered a Mr. Aiken, who was an able sailor, John Coles, sailmaker, Stephen Weeks, armorer, and two Sandwich Islanders to take the ship's pinnace out and find a channel.

The pinnace had not been gone long when she ran out a signal flag. This was a sign that she had found a passage of sufficient depth.

At once the ship weighed anchor and stood in for the channel. The *Tonquin* passed the boat but no one aboard threw a line. As the pinnace drifted astern, the passengers called frantically, "The boat, the boat, throw a line!"

"No, I will not endanger the ship," shouted the Captain.

The boat was seen for the last time struggling hard in the heavy sea to follow the ship through the breakers. When the *Tonquin* went into the shallow channel she struck again and again on the bar with shattering impact. The seas broke foaming over her in waves ten feet high. When night came on she threw out her anchor but the sea carried her steadily on toward the rocks. When all seemed lost the tide began to flow and carried the ship over the bars to the safety of deep water in Baker's Bay.

Next morning a search party was put ashore to look for survivors. Under a rocky ledge they found a naked white man. It was Weeks, the armorer who had been sent out in the pinnace. When he had somewhat revived he told his story. The boat had been overturned in the surf and Aiken and Coles had been lost. By desperate efforts the two Owyhees had righted the boat and rescued Weeks. He had then managed to secure a floating oar and had sculled the boat through breakers that carried her high up the beach. Here he found that one of the natives was dead of exhaustion; the other he had covered with leaves and left still alive by the boat.

Eight lives had been needlessly lost from the *Tonquin* when in sight of her destination.

The Interpreter's Story

As soon as they reached land the four partners hastily explored the shores of the bay and selected a commanding promontory as a site for their trading post. Everyone agreed that the new settlement should be called Astoria. Speedily, adequate shelters were built and some supplies brought ashore from the *Tonquin*. The Captain insisted on keeping aboard the greater part of the equipment and trading goods until he should return from a trading voyage which Mr. Astor had ordered him to make along the coast to Vancouver.

Ashore, the men paused for a last look at the *Tonquin* as her sails disappeared around the headlands of Cape Disappointment. Aboard the ship was Mr. Alexander McKay, one of the partners, an experienced trader. According to Mr. Astor's instructions, he was to conduct the fur trading among the Indians.

No white man ever saw the *Tonquin* or any of her crew again.

Weeks later some Indians brought in a rumor that the ship's crew had been massacred by the coastal Indians. The three remaining partners believed this to be merely a tale that was being spread among the Indians by the British Northwest Company to frighten the Astor Company.

Later an Indian came in with details of a story which he claimed he had witnessed first hand. Half spoken in broken English, half acted out in grim pantomime, the Indian told his terrible story to the Scotsmen in Astoria's log warehouse.

The Indian had been quietly fishing in a coastal inlet, he said, when the great winged canoe of the white men had picked him up. When the white men found that he spoke the languages of the coast Indians they had persuaded him to go with them as interpreter. He could speak for them to the Indians. He would be the tongue of the white man.

The ship, so the Indian told the Scotsmen, had anchored in Newetee Bay on the coast of Vancouver Island. From there the totem poles and steep roofs of an Indian village could be seen along the shore. The interpreter warned Thorn that these were bad Indians, known to be treacherous dealers.

Even as this warning was being given, canoes came alongside, and the Indians held out fine sea otter skins. These were the most valuable of all furs, but it was too late that day to trade. Some time after that, the interpreter and Mr. McKay had gone ashore to make friends with the Indians and had been entertained by the village chief. That night Mr. McKay had slept on sea otter skins of fabulous value.

The next morning when McKay and the interpreter arrived aboard the *Tonquin* she was already surrounded by canoes. Her decks were spread with trading goods, bright blankets, brass kettles, hunting knives and blue beads. In spite of this show of goods, little trading was being done, for the Indians were asking higher prices for their furs than the white men were willing to pay.

While Mr. McKay watched, a shrewd chieftain

came forward and offered Captain Thorn a pair of fine otter pelts. The Captain made what he considered a liberal offer of blankets and fish hooks. Sneering, the Indian shook his head and asked for double.

Captain Thorn was not given to arguing, especially with savages. He walked away, pacing the deck in irritation. The little savage followed him back and forth, urging his wares. He began to make gestures indicating that the Captain was stingy. Thorn turned on him in a fury and rubbed the furs in his face. As he pushed the chief over the rail he gave him a swift boot. In a rage Thorn strode down the deck, swearing and kicking furs and Indians right and left. The savages gathered up their wares and quickly disappeared over the ship's side.

The Indian interpreter came to McKay and said, "Indians very angry. Come back to kill white man. White Chief must take ship away quick."

In the Captain's cabin McKay warned there would be trouble, if he knew anything about Indians. It was dangerous, he said, to allow so many savages to come aboard the ship. The boarding nets should be put out to hold them off. Thorn laughed and pointed to the gun room, saying, "As long as we have plenty of arms we are perfectly safe. You *pretend* to know a great deal about Indian character, McKay. You *really* know nothing at all."

No more canoes came that day. Everyone but McKay spent a restful night aboard ship.

Early next morning a canoe came alongside. The Indians held up furs, making signs that they wanted to trade. Thorn was not yet on deck, but the man on watch knew that the Captain expected to trade with the Indians and so he let them climb to the deck. Several more canoes had arrived and more savages climbed over the rails. Quietly, little brown men kept appearing as if by magic.

When Thorn, McKay, and Lewis, the ship's clerk, came on deck it was swarming with Indians holding out furs. This was an agreeable sight to the Captain. If he had spoiled the market yesterday, today he would make up for it.

The Indian interpreter whispered to McKay that the savages carried weapons hidden under their short mantles. McKay noticed anxiously that the best furs were going to the sailors who passed out knives. He went to the Captain and pointed shoreward where more canoes were coming across the bay. As the perilous situation at last began to dawn on him, Thorn shouted to the mate to clear the deck, weigh anchor and hoist sail. The anchor chains rattled and half a dozen seamen climbed aloft.

Suddenly a wild yell went up and the Indians rushed upon the white men scattered about the ship. Lewis, the ship's clerk, was leaning over a bale of blankets when a savage drove a knife in his back and he fell down the companionway. As McKay leaped to his feet he was brained with a war club.

An Indian chief sprang at Thorn. The Captain drew his clasp knife and stopped him in mid-air.

Desperately Thorn fought his way toward the gun room. Bleeding from knife wounds, he leaned heavily against the steering wheel. A blow from a club knocked him to the deck. He was quickly stabbed to death and thrown overboard.

The unarmed men in the rigging dropped to the deck and four of them reached the cabin in safety. Here they found Lewis still alive. Barricading the cabin door, they opened fire on the savages and soon cleared the deck. They now turned the cannon on the canoes which were making for the shore, causing fearful damage. All day the four kept anxious watch from the gory decks of the

Tonquin as her sails flapped idly in the light breeze.

Next morning several Indian canoes put off from shore and circled the ship out of range of gun shot. There was no sign of life to be seen aboard her. When the canoes came nearer, a single figure appeared at the rail, signaled them to come aboard, and then disappeared.

After a long while a canoe ventured alongside and an Indian climbed cautiously over the rail. The decks were deserted except for the twisted corpses of the crew lying where they had fallen. Hordes of savages swarmed aboard and soon the ship was alive with excited Indians snatching at loot.

Suddenly a terrific blast split the air. A great column of water shot into the sky, followed by a billowing mushroom of smoke. Pieces of the ship, human arms, legs, and torn torsos fell back from the sky and splashed into the bay.

When the smoke cleared the *Tonquin* had utterly and forever disappeared.

The interpreter had dived overboard when the massacre began on the decks of the *Tonquin*. He had been taken into a canoe and brought back a prisoner to the Indian village. It was late on the day after the explosion when four white captives were brought in. They had been found by the Indians lying exhausted near their boat in a cove of the bay.

Before the captives were put to slow death by horrible tortures they told the interpreter what had happened aboard the *Tonquin*. After the ship had been cleared of the Indians they had dressed Lewis's wounds as best they knew. He urged them to take the ship out of the bay and down the coast to Astoria. They replied that the stiff wind that blew from the sea would surely blow her on the rocks. They would not attempt it. However, there was a chance of escape with the ship's boat. If they could row out of the bay against the wind they might work their way down the coast to Astoria. It was not a bright prospect but it was their only hope. There would be room for Lewis. He could rest comfortably in the bottom of the boat.

"Look," said Lewis, "I know I'm done for. This is the finish. I've felt it coming from away back."

He paused, lifted himself painfully on his elbow, and said feverishly, "Listen to this. After you've gone, the Indians will come back for the loot. I'll be here, I'll coax 'em aboard. I'll keep below near the powder magazine till the whole tribe is aboard. I can still navigate and I'll touch off the powder magazine."

He paused and looked at the four. "Won't that be a party?" he said eagerly. "Won't that be a show! The whole caboodle of us blown right into eternity in one grand bang—blown right to perdition on the heels of old man Thorn." He laughed feebly and fell back on his pillow. There was a long pause as the four men looked at one another.

"What a man!" said one of them. "It's a proper finish for the *Tonquin* and he's absolutely right, but we must argue him out of it."

For hours they tried to make him change his mind, but he only smiled and shook his head. It was dark now and they must leave, he told them. They made him as comfortable as they could with a jug of water and some ship's biscuit beside him. One last hand grip for good-by. Then they silently lowered the boat and the four men shoved off into the darkness.

PART II
THE OVERLAND JOURNEY

The Start
(June, 1810)

WHILE THE *Tonquin* WAS SAILING SOUTH FROM New York, Mr. Astor's overland expedition had started from Montreal. It was led by Wilson Price Hunt of Trenton, New Jersey. He was a very sensible businessman who had looked after Mr. Astor's interests in St. Louis and elsewhere for a number of years. Mr. Hunt had done his work so well that his employer had appointed him to lead the overland expedition across the American continent to the Pacific Ocean.

Hunt did not know much about living in the wilderness but he was expected to hire men who did. His discretion and agreeable temper could be counted on to smooth out the disturbances and quarrels that so often upset the course of business and the flow of profits.

And now the hiring of experienced men and the endless detail of outfitting the expedition were over. At long last Mr. Hunt and his party were clear of Montreal.

He himself sat somewhat uncomfortably exactly amidships in the forty-foot birch-bark canoe. A feeling of great relief came over him as the canoe glided over smooth waters under the steady strokes of nine voyageurs.

The Astor Company's rivals, the Northwest Company, were in control in Montreal and they had seen to it that the Astor party got off to a hard start. Hunt had been able to hire only the riffraff and castoffs of the fur trade and that at the very top wages paid in advance. He had been greatly aided by his partner Donald McKenzie, an old-time trader who with nine more voyageurs followed in Hunt's wake in a second canoe.

Day after day they followed the rivers and

crossed still lakes. At the portages where they must cross by land, the canoes and baggage were shifted to the shoulders of the voyageurs. At night they camped under the dark pines of the surrounding forest.

The arrival of Mr. Hunt's outfit at Mackinac excited the immediate and hostile interest of that straggling outpost of the Northwest Company. Here, where Lakes Michigan and Huron met, the trappers of the Canadian wilderness brought in their furs once a year and purchased or bartered supplies for the next season. From here fortunes in fur bales were paddled and portaged to Montreal and points east.

Again Mr. Hunt tried to hire experienced trappers for the party. Partisans and pork-eaters glared and shrugged off his proposals. Even his offers of top wages had no effect on the Northwesters. But Hunt was greatly encouraged when his friend Ramsey Crooks, a partner in the Astor Company, joined the outfit at this point.

One day Mr. Hunt was vainly trying to persuade a particularly wolfish-looking French-Canadian to join his party. Mr. Crooks came up and pulled out of his pocket a shining white ostrich plume. He fastened it on the battered hat of the delighted Frenchman and said, "This goes to everyone who joins up." The feather won for Mr. Hunt his first recruit! For the next few days he passed out plumes, rooster tails, and gay feathers to the voyageurs, who were now eager to sign up. But he had to pay numerous fines as well as their liquor and gambling bills before he was able to get his new employees out of town.

As the befeathered crew paddled their way westward to Prairie du Chien and down the Mississippi, Crooks insisted that the party of thirty was still too few to venture safely among the Indians of the plains. He insisted the expedition should be enlarged to at least sixty when they reached St. Louis.

St. Louis, the Arrival
(September 3, 1810)

At this time St. Louis on the Mississippi was a frontier settlement of some fourteen hundred inhabitants. Its water front was fragrant with a sour smell of animal skins from the fur warehouses. On its main street paraded a motley assembly of Yankee traders, Indian chiefs, Mississippi boatmen, trappers, and Kentucky hunters. Among its prominent citizens were old French and Spanish families. These had survived from the earlier days when the town had been at different times under both flags.

Everyone in St. Louis was interested in the fur trade. Here were outfitted the fur brigades that went up the Missouri. From here, too, supplies were sent up the river to the trading posts that Manuel Lisa had established as far as the Forks.

Lisa was the chief figure in the Missouri Fur

Company and knew more about the Indian trade than any other man in St. Louis. Through his efforts the Missouri Fur Company was planning to take over all the fur trade on the Missouri River.

However, Lisa had just had bad news from the men at his farthest outpost. Their camp at the Forks of the Missouri had been surprised by the Blackfeet. Five men had been killed and Major Andrew Henry, their leader, had disappeared in the western mountains with the survivors. Lisa was now outfitting a relief expedition which he himself would lead up the Missouri. He considered the arrival of the Astor party at this time unfortunate for his company, and he was trying to make it difficult for the rival fur company in every way possible.

As a result of Lisa's unfriendly activities, Mr. Hunt was so harassed with delays and difficulties that October arrived before he was ready to leave St. Louis. It was now too late in the season for him and his party to advance very far on their journey before winter. On the other hand, St. Louis was too hostile and expensive a place to stay. Mr. Hunt decided to leave it and winter as far up the river as he could go before bad weather set in.

Up the Missouri
(October 21, 1810)

Bucking the Big Muddy was a tough job. The river was full of dead trees, snags, and sawyers that could rip through a boat's bottom. The Missouri wound and twisted and doubled back. Its banks caved in and there were hidden sand bars.

With long poles or oars the voyageurs pushed and pulled the four barges against the strong current or scrambled along the banks, tugging at the thousand-foot cordelle, or tow rope. The long-suffering boatmen hauled the barges upstream at an average of fifteen miles a day. When there was a southeast wind a square sail helped the barges to make better time.

By November the barges had traveled four hundred and fifty miles up the Missouri, and winter was closing in. Hunt and his party built a camp of log huts at the mouth of the Nodowa River and holed in. It was good game country and everyone was satisfied.

One day two men rode into camp. They were John Day and Robert McLellan. Both were old friends of Mr. Crooks. McLellan was famous as an Indian fighter. He and Crooks had made an expedition to the fur country together but had been turned back by hostile Sioux.

The two newcomers believed that Manuel Lisa had influenced the Indians against them. Being of a violent temper, McLellan had sworn to shoot Lisa on sight. This was so agreeable to Mr. Hunt that he signed McLellan as a partner in the Astor enterprise.

Not long after the arrival of Day and McLellan, Indians came in with rumors that the Sioux were preparing to attack the Hunt party when it came up the river in the spring. The warlike tribesmen wanted to make sure that no guns or ammunition got through to their enemies, the Arikara and the Mandans farther up the river.

At this news Mr. Hunt decided to go back to St. Louis for reinforcements and for an interpreter who could speak the Sioux language. It meant a journey of about a thousand miles altogether, but he would return by spring. Beyond the Mississippi, time and distance were not serious obstacles.

Pierre Dorion

In St. Louis Hunt found that the only person there who spoke both Sioux and English was an alcoholic half-breed named Pierre Dorion. His father had been an interpreter for Lewis and Clark. The story was told that in a drunken brawl he had been on the point of scalping his own father. When the old man had appealed to Pierre's honor the dutiful son had respectfully put up his knife.

Pierre was heavily indebted to the Missouri Fur Company for a whisky bill charged at ten dollars a quart. When Lisa heard that Hunt was trying to employ Dorion, he threatened to put the law on the interpreter. Dorion, said Lisa, must either join the Missouri Fur Company or pay his debt.

This so enraged Dorion that he agreed to go with Hunt for three hundred dollars a year, two hundred of which he collected in advance. At the moment of departure he refused to leave without his Indian squaw and their two children, aged two and four. With a groan Mr. Hunt consented.

Hunt invited two British botanists, John Bradbury and Thomas Nuttall, to join the party. Their knowledge of plants and flowers would not be of much use against the Sioux but they added an air of scientific importance to the party. These gentlemen brought the news that Manuel Lisa had taken out a warrant for the arrest of Dorion. Officers of the law were awaiting him up the river at St. Charles.

On hearing this news, Dorion and his family took to the woods, leaving Mr. Hunt with the hopeless feeling of having lost his interpreter. But Mr. Hunt had given up hope too quickly. After the party left St. Charles, Dorion hailed the barges from the bank and later his squaw and children appeared.

In January, stopping at the frontier village of Charrette, Hunt talked with a noble-looking old man who came down to the river and asked many questions about the expedition. He said he was eighty-five years old, but that he was strong and active. He had just come back from a hunting trip on which he had taken sixty beaver skins. When Hunt asked his name he replied, "Daniel Boone."

Next morning they met a trapper coming downstream in a pirogue. His name was John Colter. He had traveled three thousand miles down the Missouri in thirty days.

During his wilderness journey many adventures had befallen Colter. He had taken beaver in a trapper's paradise at the headwaters of the Missouri and been robbed by the Blackfeet. He had escaped into a magical valley of boiling springs and spouting water jets at the source of the Yellowstone. He had been alone in the wilderness for over a year and now he was on his way back to see his young wife. He was excited by the new expedition and had half a mind to travel back across the Rockies with it. Never mind his new wife.

After a feast of buffalo and venison steaks the bearded travelers sat about the campfire as Colter told the story of his adventure in the land of the Blackfeet:

Early one morning, he and his companion Potts were quietly paddling up the Jefferson River to tend their traps. Suddenly they heard the dull thud of many hoofs. Colter straightened up tensely and whispered, "Indians! And Blackfeet at that! Let's vamoose!"

Potts muttered, "It's nothing but the buffler. Keep going."

In a moment the high banks were swarming with hundreds of painted warriors. An Indian signaled the two white men to come ashore. Colter swung the canoe sharply to the bank.

As Potts stepped ashore an Indian snatched his rifle. Colter leaped from the canoe, twisted the weapon out of the Indian's grasp, and handed it back to Potts.

As Potts pushed out into midstream an arrow struck him in the shoulder. "I'm wounded," he called to Colter and, lifting his rifle, he fired. An Indian dropped dead on the shore. Instantly Potts's body was filled with Indian arrows.

Colter was taken ashore, stripped naked, and tied. He could tell by their gestures that the Indians were arguing about what kind of torture would be the most painful and amusing. Presently one of the Indians asked Colter if he was a good runner. He shook his head. He was led out several hundred yards on the prairie and turned loose. With high-pitched yells the savage pack started in pursuit.

Colter ran like a jack rabbit, putting distance between himself and his pursuers. Then he settled down to a steady pace that ate up the long prairie miles. Cactus spines and sharp rocks cut his bare feet but he kept to his tireless stride. He was making for the Madison River. Instinctively he headed for running water, the friendly river that left no trace. With his mouth open, he sucked the air into his bursting lungs in great gasps. His nose was bleeding and his body was covered with his own blood.

Ahead he could see a line of cottonwoods that marked the river. Slowing a little, he looked over his shoulder. There was only one Indian anywhere near. This huge savage carried a spear and was gaining fast.

Colter suddenly stopped, turned about, and stretched out his arms as if to invite the spear thrust. As the Indian hurled his lance he stumbled and the

spear fell short and broke. Colter pounced on the pointed part of the spear and jabbed it through the fallen Indian.

Staggering on, he plunged into the river and swam out to a wooded island. Here he found a great tangle of driftwood that had been piled at the head of the island by the river current. He dived under the twisted roots and came up in a breathing space where the leaves and debris were piled thick above his head. For hours he listened to the padding footfalls of moccasined feet as the searchers came and went. What if they should set fire to the logs and brush?

Time dragged on and finally he caught a glimpse of stars shining above. He crept from his hiding place and out into the darkness. Swimming and wading down the river, he got his direction for his overland flight. Keeping to the ravines and hollows, he pushed east toward the Yellowstone River. It was spring, and he fed on the roots which he had seen the Digger Indians eat. Naked, lame, and half-starved he struggled on. After seven days he staggered into Manuel Lisa's fort on the Yellowstone.

Colter's escape from the Blackfeet is a story in the saga of the Far West that was long told at campfires on the Missouri or at the rendezvous in the "holes" and valleys of the Rockies.

On Upstream

It was late in April when the fleet again started up the Missouri. Along the banks the prairies were breaking into flower and blossom. On the wooded islands deer and buffalo browsed among the delicate green of the new leaves.

The voyageurs sang as they bent to the cordelles or poles. At the day's end, they camped on the islands where the hunters brought in savory game for the cook fires.

Each night, while the men slept, three sentinels stood guard. Stories of the ferocious Blackfeet and the savage Sioux had made the voyageurs nervous.

One night the camp was thrown into a sudden panic. Eleven Sioux warriors, stark naked, rushed into the camp brandishing tomahawks and terrifying the voyageurs. The hunters quickly rounded up the Indians at the point of their guns and were for shooting the lot of them on the spot. Mr. Hunt, thinking ahead, said such an act would make trouble for them later in the Sioux country.

Finally the Indians were rowed across the river and turned loose on the prairie with the warning that if they were seen again they would be shot. Dorion explained that they were a disappointed war party that had gone berserk.

In the Land of Danger

Hunt and his party had reached the Platte, the broad and shallow river that pours down from the Rockies, flows across the great plains, and empties into the Missouri some eight hundred miles above its mouth. The Platte was the halfway point dividing the regions known as the upper and lower Missouri. Beyond this point the river was infested by the savage Sioux who were always at war with neighboring tribes.

The Sioux got their firearms from the British. This gave them a great advantage in trade and war with the upper river tribes. It was the purpose of the Sioux to prevent the American traders from bringing goods up the river to their enemies.

Mr. Hunt was warned by the river Indians to look out for trouble from now on. In turn, Mr. Hunt warned the scientists, Bradbury and Nuttall, who persisted in wandering off into the prairies after specimens. They were sternly told not to leave the river if they wished to keep their scalps.

Across the river the party could see the teepees of an Indian encampment. It was the village of the

Omahas, composed of some eighty lodges. The Omahas had once been a numerous and powerful nation, but the Sioux and the smallpox had reduced them to some two hundred warriors.

As the travelers advanced into the Sioux country, rumors of a large band on the warpath became more alarming. The hunters kept close along the river or shot game on the islands.

Mr. Nuttall continued absent-mindedly to wander off into the prairie, returning in triumph with his "weeds," as the voyageurs called his treasured specimens. Bradbury had an even more daring talent for rambling. One May morning he decided to go on a lonely trip across the neck of a great bend in the river. It would take the barges all day to circle the bend, and he would be waiting for them, he said, when they had completed the turn.

Mr. Bradbury started off to gather specimens. Along the way he shot at several prairie dogs and missed. By mid-afternoon he stood on the river bank contentedly awaiting the barges. Suddenly he felt a hand on his shoulder. He whipped about and found himself facing a red savage with a drawn bow and the arrow pointed at his heart.

With great presence of mind, Mr. Bradbury

realized that if the Indian had wanted to murder him he would have already shot him in the back. He smiled, held out his hand and said, "How, friend." The Indian lowered his bow and took Bradbury's hand.

At this moment two other Indians leaped out of the bushes. These were not Sioux but friendly Poncas. However, they insisted on taking Mr. Bradbury with them.

The scientist flatly refused. Sitting down, he delighted his captors with the magical behavior of his pocket compass. Later he revived flagging interest with the mysteries of his microscope.

Suddenly Mr. Bradbury heard one of the Indians let out a yell and the three disappeared in the underbrush. To the scientist's immense relief he saw the barges coming around the bend. That night Mr. Bradbury recounted his adventures with satisfactory effect to an admiring circle around the campfire.

Next morning Bradbury's Indian friends appeared in company with a white stranger who said he had a message for Mr. Hunt. The message proved to be a letter from Manuel Lisa saying that he was coming upriver with a relief expedition to find Major Henry, the vanished leader of his outpost. Lisa had been trying to overtake the Hunt party for three weeks and had arrived at the Omaha village only four days after Hunt had left. (This was a record for fast travel up the river.) Lisa begged Mr. Hunt to wait for him so that their united forces could pass through the Sioux country in greater safety.

The terrible-tempered McLellan flew into a rage, saying it was one of Lisa's tricks and that he would shoot the Spanish blackguard on sight. It was finally decided to send Lisa an answer saying that the two parties should wait for each other at the Ponca village just ahead. This was merely a ruse. The Hunt party actually planned to go forward at full speed and if possible leave their dangerous rival far behind.

The Three Mountain Men
(May 26, 1810)

While the Hunt party was breakfasting next morning the lookout sighted two canoes on the other side of the river. Through a spyglass he made out three white men. A shot was fired, and the three travelers, attracted by the crack of the rifle, found their way into camp.

"Call me Robinson," said the oldest mountain man, taking off his hat and displaying a red bandana tied about his head. "The Indians lifted my hair when I was a youngster back in Kentucky and I wear the gay headgear to keep out the mosquitoes and the drafts. These two chilluns is John Hoback and Jacob Rezner." The "chilluns" nodded in silent salute.

The three grizzled trappers were from Major Henry's camp in the Rockies, where they had wintered. In the spring they had been taken with a powerful notion to see old Kentucky. They had come out of the mountains and down the Yellowstone to the Big Muddy and here they were.

The mountain men showed great interest in the Astor expedition and marveled at its excellent equipment. They were inclined to join the party and return to the mountains.

Robinson counseled that it would be better for the expedition to avoid the country of the Blackfeet. It would be safer and easier to leave the Missouri at the Arikara villages and cross the prairie to the headwaters of the Yellowstone. If they wanted to reach the Far West, he knew of a pass through the Rockies that was much easier than the one at the headwaters of the Missouri. Hunt accepted this plan and engaged the trappers as guides.

With its three new members the party moved

on toward the Arikara villages. Here they could buy plenty of horses. They would then leave the river and cross the prairie to the Stony Mountains.

Meanwhile, they could not forget that they were still passing through the country of the Sioux. Anxiously the lookout scanned the river ahead for any sign of the dreaded warriors ambushed along the bluffs of the river.

"Voilà les Sioux!"

"*Voilà les Sioux!*" cried the lookout. "There are
the Sioux!" Indian horsemen could be seen on the
high bluffs ahead and hundreds more were pouring
down from the hills beyond. There was no mis-
taking them. Through his glass Mr. Hunt could
see the piebald ponies and painted braves in full
battle array.

"*Voilà les Sioux! Voilà les Sioux!*" repeated the
frightened voyageurs. "Brother, this is no wedding
we're going to!"

The channel ahead led directly under the bluffs. It was either go ahead past the bluffs or turn back. Everything aboard that would shoot was loaded and primed. The two howitzers and the swivel gun were fired off. The reports boomed across the river and the smoke drifted downstream. The leading barge pulled toward the bluff with every man ready at his firing post.

When they came within rifle range the Indian horsemen, silhouetted against the sky, began waving buffalo robes and bringing them down to the ground.

"Don't fire," shouted Dorion. "They are making the peace sign. It is a signal that they want to parley."

As he spoke, a dozen warriors could be seen coming down the bluff to the river. At the water's edge the Indians lighted a fire and sat down in a circle. One warrior held up the peace pipe and beckoned to the barge. Hunt and the partners, heavily armed, came ashore and joined the circle.

From the bluffs above the Sioux warriors looked down silently while the pipe bearer, wearing a feather war bonnet and painted from head to foot in black-and-white stripes, stepped forward. He lifted the six-foot pipe to the sun, turned to the four points of the compass, and presented the pipe to the seated chief. After the chief had smoked, the pipe was passed around the circle in silence.

At a nudge from Dorion, Mr. Hunt now rose and made a speech in bad French. Dorion made an even worse translation into the Sioux language. He said the white men were not bringing guns to the Arikara. They were on their way to seek their white brothers where the sun sank into the sea. They had heard that the Sioux intended to oppose their passage through their country and they were prepared to resist. He hoped that the Sioux would not make war, for the white men wished to be their friends and had brought them presents. Here Dorion passed out fifteen carrots of tobacco and several bags of corn.

The Sioux chief now rose and delivered a long and magnificent speech. He saw that the white men were not bringing aid to his enemies. The Sioux would not attack the travelers, for it was good that they should seek their white brothers beyond the mountains. He thanked the strangers for their presents. It would be well if they would camp on the other side of the river. His young men were wild and restless and might cause trouble.

After the chief finished speaking, everyone rose and shook hands. The Indian horsemen rode off into the hills.

That night around the camp fires the voyageurs rejoiced. The trappers were relieved. It was a victory without bloodshed. They could now pass through the Sioux country in safety.

Manuel Lisa Catches Up
(June 2, 1810)

Next day while Hunt's barge was backing off a sand bar, he heard the warning signal gun fired from the barge across the river. A band of Indians in war paint came streaming down out of the hills to the river's edge. For a few minutes Hunt thought this was Sioux treachery, but the Indians turned out to be an Arikara and Mandan war party on the warpath against the Sioux. After a friendly parley both sides settled for a feast and celebration.

A barge was now sighted pulling upstream. She manned twenty oars and a swivel gun. It could be no one but Manuel Lisa. The rival traders, Hunt and Lisa, greeted each other sourly. McLellan practically had to be tied to prevent him from shooting Lisa. The two parties camped near each other in a heavy rainstorm.

Lisa asked Dorion aboard his barge to sample some whisky. Over the bottle he suggested that this was a good time for Dorion to come on over to the Missouri Fur Company, where he belonged. When Dorion refused, Lisa reminded him of the whisky bill he still owed the company. Dorion went ashore in a fury and reported the affair to Hunt.

In the midst of Dorion's story Lisa appeared at the tent door merely to borrow a tow line, or so he said. In a few moments Lisa and Dorion were exchanging threats, and Dorion poked Lisa violently in the nose. Lisa rushed out of the tent looking for a weapon.

News of the row had spread through the camps and Crooks and McLellan rushed into Hunt's tent with their rifles, seeking Lisa. That gentleman now appeared, brandishing a large butcher knife, and rushed at Dorion, who snatched Hunt's pistols and pointed them at Lisa.

Mr. Hunt, who had been trying to keep Mc-

Lellan from committing murder, now interfered between Lisa and Dorion. In the heat of the argument Lisa implied that Mr. Hunt's ancestors had been coyotes. This remark could never be made safely on the upper Missouri without a smile, and Lisa did not smile.

Hunt was now the maddest man in camp and instantly challenged Lisa to a duel. Lisa ran back to his barge for pistols. Mr. Bradbury had been looking on at the whole affair from the detached point of view of the botanist. He now decided it was time that he took a hand in it, and he succeeded with considerable difficulty in arranging an armed truce. On these terms both parties advanced on the Arikara villages.

Arikara Horses

In the Arikara camp the warriors had gathered at Chief "Big Man's" lodge. Inside, the great chief himself sat in the semi-darkness. A column of light fell from the smoke hole in the top of the lodge and lighted his savage features as he spoke.

Manuel Lisa and Mr. Hunt eyed each other grimly across the council circle. They had not spoken since the Dorion row.

Slowly the peace pipe went round the council circle. "Big Man" ended his welcoming speech with some remarks about the poverty of his people. This was obviously an invitation for bids from the rival white chiefs.

Lisa rose and began to speak. This was an uncomfortable moment for Mr. Hunt. Lisa had traded with the Arikara before and was held in high esteem by them. If he influenced the Indians against him, Hunt would get no horses for the overland expedition.

Lisa began with the usual trader's sales talk of friendship and gave a glittering list of the fine things he had to trade. He ended by explaining that the Hunt party was a tribe entirely separate from his own. However, he added, any insult or harm done them by the Indians he would consider as done to himself.

"I trust," he said, "that you will show them the same friendship you have always shown toward me." Then he added handsomely, "I also hope that you will do everything to help and assist them on their way."

Mr. Hunt gasped with surprise. By a master stroke of diplomacy Lisa had satisfied everybody.

Hunt now addressed the Indians and said he desired to trade for horses so that he might proceed across the mountains to his white brothers on the great salt water. The usual presents of tobacco were distributed to the Indians.

After the speeches Hunt and Lisa shook hands warmly. Lisa even offered to trade a fair number of his horses for Mr. Hunt's barges which would have to be left on the river anyway.

The three camps now got down to business in the Indian sign language. To show the good quality of their horses, the lithe red riders put the piebald mustangs through their paces on the prairie beyond the Indian village. The Arikara were born and bred on horseback. Men, women, and children were splendid riders. The Kentucky trappers missed none of the fine points of the Indians' superb horsemanship. Hunt purchased eighty-two horses.

While the trading went on, Indian women dressed in white deerskin stood by in chattering groups. Some were tall and handsome with a lithe, mysterious beauty that was not lost on the French voyageurs. Dozens of naked children and wolfish dogs darted to and fro.

During this time, the camp was in a continual state of excitement. Rumors of the Sioux war parties in the neighborhood were reported daily. Bands of Arikara warriors armed with bows, spears, and shields came and went in flashing splendor of paint and feathers. The whole tribe swayed and leaped and stamped for hours to the rhythm of Indian drums in the War or Scalp or Buffalo Dance.

The trappers watched a victorious war party ride into camp amid a wild tumult of rejoicing. At the head of the procession rode a magnificent young brave. He was mortally wounded but sat his horse with a calm face. That night in the lulls of the frenzied victory chants, the wails of the mourners for the war dead rose on the hills above the camp.

In Hunt's camp the baggage was carefully inspected, ready for the following day's departure on the long journey across the unknown western plains.

Shoving Off
(July 18, 1811)

It was mid-July. As the sun rose over the rim of the treeless horizon the long procession moved slowly out onto the rolling prairie. Most of their eighty-two horses carried the ammunition, provisions, Indian goods, and traps that made up the baggage of the expedition. The partners were all mounted, and Dorion rode a lean mustang. Behind him trudged his squaw and the two children. The rest of the company marched on foot in Indian file, carrying their personal equipment.

Lisa gaily waved his hat in farewell, remarking hopefully that the whole expedition would either starve to death in the mountains or be scalped by the Crows and Blackfeet. He was glad the Missouri was clear of the rival company.

If the Blackfeet were specialists in murder, the Crows had earned a reputation for thieving and horse stealing of which they were proud. This native talent they had developed into a pastime, a profession, and a fine art.

It was across the country of this tribe that the expedition was now advancing. To the men who had come from the dark eastern forests, this treeless country of rolling plains was utterly strange. For days and weeks they marched on, bewildered by the dazzling light of the broiling summer sun.

But the trappers of the upper Missouri, who lived in this wilderness, carried in their minds a picture map of its ranges and river courses. Over these they wandered with an unfailing sense of direction. In the slightest print of foot or hoof they could read whole biographies. They could tell the age, size, color, destination, thoughts, and fears of any creature who had passed. They were versed in the mysterious lore of this enchanted land, and the

spell of its boundless freedoms had forever possessed them. In the hunter's camp, in lonely green valleys, and in the wild rush of the buffalo hunt, the trapper found rich compensations for all his dangers and privations.

Hunting on the rolling prairie, the trappers brought in buffalo, elk, bear, and antelope meat for the cook fires. Full-gorged on the tender hump of buffalo cow, the men wiped their greasy beards on their bloodstained hunting shirts and in the red glow of the campfire told tall tales to the music of the wolf and the coyote's howl.

Week after week the long procession tramped across the empty prairie toward the sunset. Skirting the Black Hills, they advanced toward the distant Big Horn Mountains.

By September they had come four hundred miles across the prairies from the Missouri. At night there was frost and the water froze. Through the clear thin air of the high barren plateaus they could see mountains that were still a hundred miles away. This was the Big Horn range, the first bastion of the fabulous Stony Mountains, across whose fearful peaks they must perilously pass.

Wearily they climbed up the bleak defiles of a

barren world that was utterly strange to both river- and plainsmen, and slid down rocky slopes into the valley of the Big Horn River. Here they again found green grass and buffalo herds. With a new supply of jerked meat they pushed on and reached the Wind River on September 9.

It was blowing cold and they began to feel the teeth of the mountain winter. The three trappers who had guided them from the Missouri said that if they followed the Wind River they would have only one mountain range to cross before reaching the headwaters of the Columbia. But supplies were getting low and there would be no game in the mountains ahead. After following the Wind River for eighty miles they turned off on an Indian trail that seemed to lead in the right direction.

As the travelers came out on the summit of a ridge, known later as Union Pass, a vast panorama spread out beneath them. Range on range of jagged peaks reached to the sky. The guides pointed to the farthest horizon where three snow-white peaks shone dimly—the Tetons. Beyond these, the guides said, lay the headwaters of the Columbia. For the moment it seemed that the end was almost in sight and the travelers' spirits rose.

They scrambled on down into the lush Green River valley and came upon grazing buffalo herds. There was the frenzied orgy of a buffalo hunt— a horse race, a cavalry charge and a bullfight all in one. There was the butchering of a fine kill, followed by an unaccustomed feast. Then the men rested while they dried the meat and made pemmican against the lean days ahead.

For a few more days the party remained in this lonely green paradise in the heart of the Rockies. The awesome beauty and timeless peace of this Arcadian valley on the roof of the world seemed to whisper "stay here always."

But they must go forward again to scale the mountain walls and follow westward-flowing waters that rushed madly through deep canyons toward the distant sea. Again the long procession of men and pack horses filed westward on the steep ascent.

In the Heart of the Rockies
(Henry's Fort, October 8, 1811)

It was a terrifying world of granite walls and peaks. The party stumbled on, following the stream that led them to a fork where two torrents cascaded into a sizable river which flowed furiously westward. To this river they gave the unpromising name Mad River. It was later to be known as the Snake.

The party camped on its banks, believing they had reached the headwaters of the Columbia. Perhaps they could paddle canoes down this very stream to the great Columbia itself. The voyageurs were weary of climbing precipices and they looked at the river with a deep desire.

Everywhere there was sign of beaver. Hunt called for volunteers. He organized a trapping party, provided them with traps and supplies and sent them into the mountains for the fall hunt. The trapping party was to come down the Columbia and join the rest of the party in the spring.

Most of those who remained with Hunt were for getting into canoes and shooting easily down to the Columbia at once. Axmen set to work cutting pines from which pirogues were to be hollowed out.

Mr. Hunt sent a scouting party down the Mad River to see how the going was. In a few days the men returned, saying that the river had kept getting madder and that canoes would be unable to navigate its furious rapids. The Indians said this was true.

The three Henry trappers—Robinson, Hoback, and Rezner—now came forward with the report that Major Henry's mountain retreat was somewhere in the neighborhood. They could easily lead the party to it. This place would make a base for their final push to the Pacific. The disappointed voyageurs again shouldered their packs and followed the worn horses westward over the high Teton pass. Pressing on, they came to a stream a hundred yards wide. This was the north fork of the Snake River. On its banks they discovered the abandoned cabins of Henry's fort.

Here Major Henry had retreated after the Blackfeet had attacked his post at the Three Forks of the Missouri. This fort of the Missouri Fur Company was the first trading post to be established west of the Continental Divide. Henry and his trappers spent a lean winter in this mountain retreat and in the spring of 1811 abandoned the fort. Breaking up into small parties, they returned eastward by various routes. Henry himself made his way to the Missouri, where he found Lisa at the Arikara villages.

Hunt now planned to make this abandoned fort a trading post of the Pacific Fur Company.

Caldron Linn
(October 28, 1811)

Here on the banks of the Snake a difficult decision must be made. Should the expedition with its horses and baggage continue by land or should they abandon the horses and continue on down the Snake in canoes? From here on the river would be their only guide.

The voyageurs urged that the party abandon the horses and take to the pirogues which they, the voyageurs, would make from tree trunks. They were sure these would carry the party swiftly and safely down the Snake to the Pacific. Mr. Hunt was not at all sure about this but finally yielded to the majority. The horses were left in charge of two Snake Indians to be redeemed later. Robinson, Rezner, and Hoback were to remain here and trap through the winter, coming down to the coast in the spring.

In ten days fifteen great tree trunks had been shaped into the long pirogues. These were now loaded with the baggage, and the expedition embarked on the rushing current in high spirits with cheers and a boat song.

At first all was smooth sailing but after a few days the course of the river became rocky and dangerous. The pirogues raced desperately through wild cataracts and down rock-strewn rapids. In this surging torrent, Crooks' canoe struck a rock and capsized. All but the steersman, Antoine Clappine, managed to reach safety. Poor Clappine was carried downstream and drowned.

The party halted at a point where the river plunged into a narrow gorge whose rocky walls rose two and three hundred feet above the water. A scouting party sent ahead to examine the channel returned reporting that it was absolutely impassable. Gloomily they christened the place "The Caldron Linn," or "The Devil's Blow Hole."

The expedition must now go on through an un-known wilderness without guides and with very little food. Winter was fast approaching. In spite of whatever might lie ahead, they must now travel on foot, packing their equipment on their backs.

Three small parties, McLellan with three men, McKenzie with five, and John Reed, the clerk, went ahead. They later united and found their way to the Columbia. The heavier baggage was labo-riously buried in nine caches.

The main body now divided into two parties. One band of eighteen men under Crooks pro-ceeded down the left bank of the river. Led by Hunt, the other party of twenty-two persons, in-cluding the Dorion family, took the right bank. Ahead of them lay a thousand miles of wilderness no white man had ever crossed.

On November 9th the two parties started on their long hunger march. Occasionally they met a few half-starved Snake Indians with whom they traded for a lean pack horse or a little food. When there was nothing else they chewed on tough beaver skins and their worn moccasins. For weeks the weary men staggered along the banks and through rocky gorges of the Snake River.

Hunt's party came to a narrow canyon where the walls rose sheer from the water and through which they could find no passage. Climbing up the shoulder of the mountain, Hunt gazed desperately across the snow-covered ranges to the horizon. There was no way ahead. They must turn back and find another way.

As they started back, they heard someone across the river shouting in English. It was Crooks and his men, so lean with hunger that they were scarcely recognizable. The two parties turned back on opposite banks of the river.

Hunt's party was the first to find food when they came upon a group of Indian lodges. The savages fled, but the white men captured five of their horses. One of these was immediately killed and cooked. A bull boat, made from the horse's hide, was used to ferry meat to the starving men watching on the opposite shore. Already they had built fires and heated their water kettles.

One Canadian named Provost, crazed by the smell of the cooking meat from across the river, climbed into the returning bull boat. In midstream he began to clap his hands and dance, upsetting the coracle. He was drowned in the swift current.

Farther on, Hunt learned from a band of Shoshone Indians that to the northwest in the Blue Mountains he would find a pleasant valley called the Grande Ronde. Here there dwelt hospitable Indians who had many horses. These Indians would guide him to the Columbia. From the Shoshones Hunt procured a little food and an Indian guide.

Four exhausted Canadians remained behind with the Shoshones. They were told to find Crooks and his young companion John Day. These two had become too ill to go on and so had been left behind on the banks of the Snake to find their way to the Columbia as best they could.

On December 24th the expedition started across the wilderness in a northwest direction. The voyageurs were glad to be leaving the Snake River at last. They had traveled eight hundred miles along its banks.

The party staggered on behind their five lean pack horses, leaning into the bitter wind that brought snow and rain as they marched on. Dorion asked that he and his family be allowed to drop behind and overtake them later.

Struggling on through the rugged hills, the party

came upon a long valley where the sun was warm. This was the Grande Ronde of which the Indians had spoken. By a pleasant stream they could see a Shoshone encampment. Here the worn travelers camped. From the Indians Hunt procured a few horses and dogs and of these the men made the first full meal they had eaten in many days.

Next day Dorion arrived. On his bony nag proudly sat his squaw with her newborn baby in her arms. During the long cruel journey she had cared for her family and borne her part with heroic endurance.

On the following morning, as preparations were made to continue the march, the voyageurs came to Mr. Hunt. "Today is the New Year," they said. "At our houses in Montreal it is a day for singing and dancing. Will the Commandant grant us a holiday?"

"You've earned it, my brave friends," said Mr. Hunt, and added with a grin, "Go to it, boys, and for today the devil take Mr. Astor and all his beavers!"

As the sun came up over the mountains like a red tomato, the voyageurs leaped up with a mighty yell. They kicked their heels to the big blue sky in a three times ring-around-a-rosy to the tune of "Buffalo Girls." They ate an enormous breakfast. Then the frolic began. They danced "The Grizzly Bear" and "The Beaver Wiggle," "The Starvation Waltz" and "The Dog Stew Fling," "The Big Horn Reel" and "The Missouri Polka."

For lunch they ate a boiled wolf and then the fun really started. The Shoshone braves stood on the sidelines and grinned. They too were dancers and they knew style when they saw it. Their black-haired squaws laughed out loud and clapped in rhythm. The wolf dogs sang, the west wind moaned, and the mountains roared. The Snake River threw several extra loops and the beavers slapped their tails in chorus. The trappers rolled on their backs and the mountain men hollered for joy, while Mr. Hunt sang "Columbia, the Gem of the Ocean" in a growling bass.

That night they chewed horse steaks and dipped their fingers in a fat dog stew. When the moon came up, the mountain men told tall tales and laughed till their lean ribs rattled and ached. Then they rolled up in their buffalo robes and snored like bears under the burning stars.

The New Year's Day frolic cheered everyone

99

immensely, and they now tackled the last and toughest range of the Blue Mountains. Over fallen trees and through waist-deep snow they slowly fought their way across the terrible mountain wilderness. They came perilously down the last defile between stupendous ridges and out upon a warm and broad plain. Around the Indian camp in the middle of the plain the travelers' hungry eyes spied hundreds of horses.

Here deep sadness fell upon the party. Dorion's baby died from exposure, and one of the straggling Canadian voyageurs disappeared and was never found.

As the party feasted and rested among the friendly Indians, Hunt learned that he was on the Umatilla River near where it joined the Columbia. The Indians told him that white men had recently gone down the river. Hunt guessed that these must have been McLellan, Reed and McKenzie and their men. With a deep thrill he noticed that the Indians had brass kettles and iron hatchets, showing they had traded with Europeans. Hunt knew that his men's troubled wanderings were ending; their grim journey was nearly over. They were nearing the promised land.

The Arrival
(February 15, 1812)

There it lay before them at last—the Columbia, wide and clear, rushing between its rocky banks to the sea. The Indians ferried the Astor party across to the north bank. From there Hunt and his men marched westward, trading with the shrewd and thievish river tribes who had learned the wily ways of the white traders of the Oregon coast.

The travelers marveled at the quantities of salmon drying on the fish racks. At the trading village of Wishram they saw the well-built houses of the Oregon Indians, with their steep roofs and floors sunk six feet below the level of the ground.

Hunt was told by the Indians about a log fort that had recently been built by white men at the mouth of the Columbia. From the Indians he heard reports of the *Tonquin* massacre. These he rejected as mere rumors.

Farther on the party came to the "Long Narrows" or "Dalles," the most dangerous stretch of water on the river.

Here, after some hard bargaining, they purchased canoes—light, long craft hollowed from fifty-foot tree trunks. For several days the voyageurs shot dangerous rapids and crossed difficult portages. At last the canoes swept out into the great bay of the Columbia where the river met the ocean.

They could smell the sea and faintly hear the roar of breakers. Their muscles tensed and the stroke of the paddles quickened. Hunt's thoughts too were racing. Would there be only the sea and the forest to greet them? Had the *Tonquin* made it? Would they find a fort or had the Indians . . .

His eyes anxiously searched the dark shores. As the canoes cleared a headland, there it was—or was it? For a moment the men stared open-mouthed and breathless. Then a wild shout broke whooped, and the partners joined in the wild frolic.

In spite of hunger and high water, the unbeatable Astorians had crossed the continent from Montreal and New York to the Pacific and sailed around the Americas to keep their rendezvous with destiny in the log fort under the Stars and Stripes at the mouth of the Columbia.

hoarsely across the water, followed by high-pitched yells. The voyageurs cheered again and again as they fiercely swung their paddles. Their eyes were riveted on the distant opening in the trees where the log fort stood on a headland etched against the sky.

From the flag pole they could see the Stars and Stripes being run up, and as the colors broke out on the breeze, cheers answered back over the water. As the canoes hit the beach, every gun in the fort was barking a salute. The voyageurs wept, embraced, leaped into the air, and danced.

The dour faces of the Scotsmen at the fort spread with broad grins, and then they threw back their heads and shook the forests with roars of welcome. Old trappers pounded each other on the back as they screeched the Indian war whoop.

As Mr. Hunt stepped ashore he was greeted by McKenzie, McLellan, and Reed, who had left him at Caldron Linn and who had reached Astoria nearly a month before. Each had stories to tell of the long stark journey, but these could wait till tomorrow. Tonight they would celebrate.

After the feasting, songs and toasts, the fiddles tuned up. The voyageurs danced, the trappers

Astoria
(1812)

The giant spruce trees in the dripping forests of the Northwest had been saplings when Abraham first journeyed westward from the land of the Chaldees four thousand years ago. The white fog from the Pacific shrouded their great trunks in silence and in mystery. On the great bar that extended across the bay from the dim headland of Cape Disappointment, the surf roared, and the never-ending rain drummed on the roofs of the cabins at Fort Astoria. Winter on the coast of Oregon was a dim, sad, lonely time.

Before the roaring fire in the big hall, Duncan McDougal told in his thick Scotch burr the bitter story of the *Tonquin's* voyage and repeated the Indian's tragic narrative of the massacre. Sprawling on the rough furniture, shaggy men listened grimly.

On other nights Hunt told the long saga of the crossing of the continent from Montreal. Three thousand five hundred miles in three hundred and forty days! Each day and mile had been sharply etched on his memory. With an odd exactitude he had figured that the journey from the Missouri was seventeen hundred and fifty-one miles.

Hunt listened with especial interest to the story of what had happened at Astoria before his arrival:

The axmen had attacked the giant trees and soon had erected the cabins and fort. The men had worked through the summer, strengthening Astoria's defenses and organizing for the fur trade. On June 15 two vagabond Indian women, disguised as men, had brought news from the upper Columbia that the Northwest Company had established a trading post in that region. This was disturbing news. It meant that Mr. Astor's Pacific Fur

Company would soon have to compete with the westward drive of the great British company.

In July David Stuart, one of the partners who had come on the *Tonquin*, organized a fur brigade for a five-hundred-mile journey up the Columbia. His purpose was to establish a trading post at Okanagan to meet possible competition from the northwesters.

As Stuart's party was about to leave, a strange canoe arrived at the fort from upriver. In it were David Thompson, trapper and astronomer, with a party of nine Northwesters and the British flag. He had crossed the Canadian wilderness in a bold attempt to beat the Astorians to the Columbia and had lost out only by a bare three months.

Thompson was looked on with suspicion by all the partners except McDougal, who welcomed this rival and supplied him for his return trip. On July 23, Stuart and Thompson started up the Columbia.

Meanwhile a stout palisade had been built about the fort with protecting bastions mounting four cannon. It was none too soon. When the terrible fate of the *Tonquin* became known, the hostile tribes of coastal Indians began to gather in the vicinity of the fort.

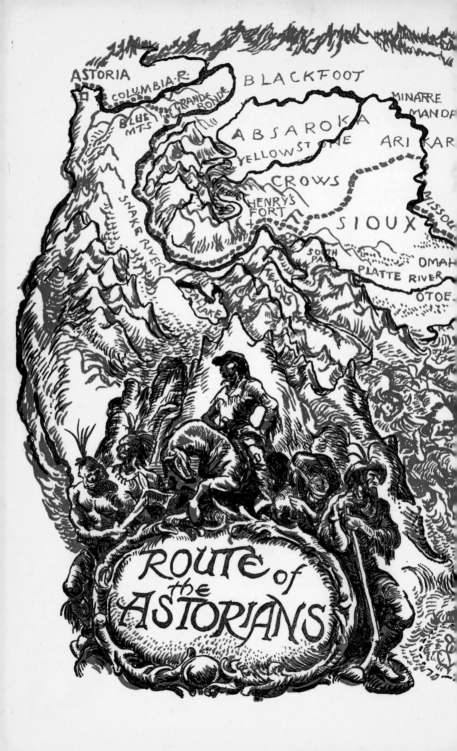

ROUTE of the ASTORIANS

McDougal called a council of the chiefs of these threatening Indians. He showed them a small bottle. In it, he said, was the demon of the smallpox. If the Indians made war on the white men he would loose the demon from the bottle and the terrible scourge would destroy their people. The terrified chiefs made peace, which they faithfully kept.

In the fall a fur brigade had been sent out to hunt in the Willamette Valley, which was found to be teeming with beaver.

The year 1811 had been successful for Mr. Astor's enterprise. New Year's Day, 1812, was celebrated with good cheer and high hopes. On a rainy January day a ragged, half-starved band of wanderers had arrived at the fort. They were McKenzie, McLellan, Reed, and eight men who had left Hunt's party at Caldron Linn.

As Mr. Astor's appointed representative, Mr. Hunt now assumed command of the fort in place of the unpopular McDougal. With the coming of spring, the Astorians' lean diet of game was increased with salmon, sturgeon and smelt. Also, the good weather now made it possible for a messenger to cross the mountains with a report to Mr. Astor of the establishment of the post on the Pacific.

On March 22 John Reed, the tall and fearless Irishman, started up the Columbia on this errand. The message to Mr. Astor was in a bright tin box strapped to his back. This shining object attracted the interest of the Indians. Mr. Reed was promptly knocked on the head with a war club and the tin box disappeared. The Irishman was a hard-headed man, however, and soon recovered.

Reed returned to Astoria with David Stuart's party, which was coming down the river from Okanagan, where Stuart had been successful in establishing a trading post.

Along the river Stuart and Reed picked up two white men who had just been robbed by the Columbia River Indians. They were stark naked and destitute of food or arms. The strangers turned out to be Ramsay Crooks and John Day, who with four Canadians had been left among the Snake Indians. After spending a winter of incredible hardship in the mountains, these two had made their way to the Columbia and with wilderness luck had in their darkest hour sighted Stuart's canoes.

When Stuart's party reached Astoria on May 11 it found the settlement in high spirits. On the

day before, the ship *Beaver* had arrived, six months to a day out of New York, with a cargo of supplies and reinforcements led by a young man named John Clark.

Greatly heartened by the arrival of the *Beaver*, a band of sixty men led by Clark, David Stuart, and McKenzie started up the Columbia to establish trading posts in the interior.

PART
III
THE
RETURN
EAST

Upstream

THE SEVEN MEN IN THE DUGOUT CANOE SWUNG
their paddles in perfect rhythm and each stroke in
unison drove the pirogue forward against the
strong current. They were silent, putting their
strength into their work, for the Columbia was
running spring flood and making progress against
its power took all a strong man had to give.

Within sight were nine other canoes and two
barges manned with oars, all pulling upstream
steadily. There were sixty men in the expedition
leaving Astoria, divided into three brigades, each

assigned to its special mission in the Columbia back country. The seven men in the canoe were assigned to the most perilous mission of all, for they were setting out for St. Louis over the wild route that Hunt had followed westward so hazardously.

Robert Stuart, their leader, carried the dispatches containing a report of the expedition for Mr. Astor—the first account of the founding and progress of the post at Astoria. Stuart was the only one in his party who had not crossed with Hunt, as he had come by sea on the *Tonquin*. (It was he who had compelled Captain Thorn at pistol's point to turn back for the boat abandoned at the Falkland Islands.) Because of his clear-headed resolution he had been selected by Hunt to lead the return expedition.

Ramsay Crooks knew from terrible experiences that crossing the Rockies was no picnic, but he was determined to return to civilization and so had joined the party. Out of loyalty, his inseparable companion John Day was reluctantly accompanying him. Robert McLellan was so temperamentally strong and wrong-headed that he too was returning. The other three men were adventurers with itching feet who craved excitement and danger.

They were approaching the Dalles and the Long Narrows where the piratical Indians of Wishram would be waiting along the shore to rob, attack or loot as opportunity provided. Each man was alerted for action and assigned his post at the portage which they were approaching. With military precision the boats were unloaded, the baggage packed for four miles, and the boats expertly hauled up the cataract. Shore guards with pointed rifles coolly held back the threatening crowds of frustrated Indians.

The whole operation was accomplished with expert coordination by men who were master craftsmen of operating in the wilderness. This maneuver was repeated at the Dalles, or Long Narrows. Above these the river was smoother and the canoes made better time.

In one month they reached the mouth of the Walla Walla just below the forks of the Columbia. Here Stuart procured twenty horses from the friendly Walla Wallas, who welcomed the white men and their own extinction with songs and dances and savage hospitality. Stuart obtained a spirited horse, a magnificent animal which he promised himself he would present to Mr. Astor.

At the camp that night a band of Indians came in to trade. John Day leaped up shouting and rushed upon them, cursing, swearing and shaking his fists. He raged on in a senseless fury. It was plain that he was out of his mind.

"These are the Indians that robbed us last year," said Crooks. "It was the last straw after a winter of starvation. It broke him down. I don't think he has been right in the head since. Seeing them again has brought on another attack."

Day finally subsided in a pitiful sobbing, saying he was sorry and that he didn't know what he was doing.

In the early hours of the morning the camp was roused by a pistol shot and then another. After the commotion it was found that Day had fired the pistols in an attempt to take his own life. He was violently and hopelessly deranged by the prospect of repeating the terrible suffering of another wilderness journey. He was sent back to Astoria under guard of trustworthy Indians, and the six other men went on.

Water of Life

Stuart and his men rode gallantly out on the great plains as their companions waved and yelled farewell.

Their blood beat quick with the spirit of high adventure and dangerous wayfaring. They were crossing the great sandy plain of the Columbia. Far on the edge of the southern horizon shimmered faintly in the heat haze the ranges of the Blue Mountains. The sun climbed in the fiery sky and beat down in scorching rays. Occasionally a little breeze blew clouds of white sand from the crest of the dunes, stinging the men's parched nostrils and throats and caking their cracked lips. The land was baked and desolate. No living thing grew.

Hour after hour they filed across the blazing desert. Gradually the horses' heads drooped wearily and the men slumped in their saddles. A craving thirst tortured man and beast. The little procession staggered on through the furnace of the long afternoon, hopelessly scanning each dry ravine for water.

Late in the afternoon Stuart halted. "Look," he pointed. "Trees." On the horizon was a faint line of smudge. They were the cottonwoods that always grew on the banks of running water.

The little brigade came alive. The horses lifted their heads and with ears thrown forward quickened their pace. The sun went down in a red mist; a cooling breeze sprang up as darkness came on. Presently the horses caught the scent of water and broke into a gallop. It was midnight when they rode up to the bank and plunged belly-deep into the cool stream. The horses thrust their muzzles in and drank long, lifting their heads, snorting and dipping in again to drink. The men threw themselves down on the bank, their heads in the water, and gulped long draughts. Again and again they dipped to drink and, finally picketing their horses, lay down and slept.

The Three Musketeers

First thing next morning everybody again drank deep of the wondrous water and had a cooling swim. The little river was the Umatilla. They had come across forty-five miles of desert to its welcoming banks.

Today they were plunging into the Blue Mountains. They were soon scrambling up their steep slopes under the cool pine trees. They struggled up the steep ravines filled with boulders and fallen trees. Every muscle of horse and man was brought into play as they clawed and hauled their way up almost perpendicular walls. The effort was wild and exciting and they were soon panting over the top and down the other side. They came out into gently rolling hills and pleasant meadows with streams that wandered into a placid lake. This was the Grande Ronde, a sort of garden of Eden in the wilderness. No wonder the Indians loved it. It was a place for trappers to live and dream forever.

Beyond the Grande Ronde they came out on a level plain criss-crossed by files of cottonwood trees following the hidden streams. As they crossed this expanse they saw a band of antelope, or goats, as the trappers called them. These dainty creatures darted with birdlike speed across the landscape and disappeared.

At last the party drew up on the sandy banks of the Snake where, 400 yards wide, it rushed into impassable mountain ranges. For six of the party the Snake carried terrible memories and yet they were ready to assay its rugged way again. The spirit of young adventure called and they were ready to follow its grim and winding course.

All the more so when they picked up a lone Indian who said that there was a white man living with his tribe a day's journey upstream. It must be one of Hunt's men, the travelers decided, and they were eager to reclaim this lost soul from a fate that had been so nearly their own.

After two days' travel they reached an encampment of Snake Indians who said there were white men across the river. But an Indian messenger who was sent over came back saying there were none.

Through the hot nights the mosquitoes plagued the travelers and the fierce flies tormented the horses by day. "All Indians are liars," Stuart concluded, and determined to press on to the cache at Caldron Linn.

Next day the band encountered another lone lean Indian. He rushed up and began embracing and petting Stuart's beautiful horse. The animal responded by rubbing his muzzle against the Indian in evident affection. It was apparently a reunion. The Indian said the horse was his and had been stolen by the Walla Walla. This did not interest Stuart in the least. As the rest of the party came up they recognized the Indian as one of Hunt's guides. Stuart proposed that he become their guide. The members of the party each offered an inducement—a knife, a hatchet, a blanket—in all an Indian fortune. The Indian now said he would show them a short cut saving miles and days. What with all the palaver the party made but nine miles that day.

Next morning the Indian and Stuart's prized animal were gone. Stuart was heartbroken. The rest of the party cursed all Indians and said the only good ones were dead ones.

Next day they followed the bend of the Snake. As the heat grew intense the men waited for two of the party to go to the river and fill the canteens.

When they reached the bluff above the river, one of the men said, pointing, "Look! An Indian under the willow trees."

"An Indian your grandmother! Did you ever see an Indian with a long black beard?" said his companion. "It's a white man! Hi! Below there!" he yelled.

The man crouching by the water jumped as if shot. "Waugh! Whoopee! Ki Yi!" he screeched, dancing and waving his arms as he rushed up the bank. At the same time three figures appeared from under the willows and came charging up.

"Raise my hair, if it ain't Robinson," bawled Crooks. "And Hoback—and Rezner—and Miller," as each man came up.

"I reckon when I git to St. Peter's gate you three'll be standing there looking natural as sin," Mr. Stuart said, beaming.

"More like when you get to the burning pit they'll be standing there grinning like wildcats," roared McLellan.

After the hand shaking and laughter had subsided Hoback said, "We ain't et for several months. 'Most forgotten how, but if you got a chaw of jerky in your fixin's we'd certainly like to try our teeth on it."

The four men sat and wolfed the elk meat which their comrades provided. At camp that night they told a fabulous tale of wilderness adventure. From Caldron Linn they had wandered south following a river (the Bear) teeming with beaver and taking many pelts. After two hundred miles they had come to a vast stretch of salt water, the Pacific Ocean (really the Great Salt Lake). From here they had gone due east two hundred miles, and had met a large band of Arapahoes who had robbed them of everything except their arms and shirts. They had holed in for the winter and with spring had again taken up the march with two pack horses which the Arapahoes had left them.

As there was absolutely no game they had lived by fishing. It was hardly living, because there were times when there were no fish. Their sufferings had been indescribably horrible. They supposed they had come some hundred miles. It was only by the luck of the wilderness that they had been found by Stuart's party.

"What about Cass? Where is he?"

"The dog stole our last horse and absconded. We ain't seen him since." There was a gleam in the shifting savage eyes of the man who said this, and it made Stuart wonder if both Cass and his horse had not been eaten by the starving survivors.

The four trappers now joined Stuart's party, saying they had had enough of the mountains and would be glad to go on to St. Louis with them.

The band of ten now followed the Snake through a land as barren and fantastic as the mountains of the moon. The salmon were coming up the Snake, and at the Falls the Indians were spearing and drying them by the thousands. The travelers traded with the Indians for a supply of dried salmon that provided food for their journey through the barren deserts that lay ahead.

Riding up to the rim of the gloomy canyon, the travelers dismounted and peered down into the foaming waters below. This was it, the Caldron Linn where Clappine had been lost.

"There's the wrecked canoe," said Stuart, pointing to the smashed dugout wedged under a rocky ledge.

For a few moments they were silent, each man thinking his own sad thoughts.

"Let's go," said McLellan, breaking the somber spell. "The cache is near here. Let's find it."

It took no scouting to find the place, for they soon came upon six gaping holes where the supplies had been buried the previous fall. Not a single bale had been left by the plunderers. There was plenty of Indian sign and wolf tracks, too. Perhaps the wolves, scenting the hides, had opened the caches and thus the Indians had found them. There were a few papers and company records scattered about.

Crooks and McLellan began circling and examining the ground to find the three remaining caches. In a few minutes Crooks was digging with his knife. "Yah! Here we are," he whooped as he dragged several beaver traps from a skin-covered bale. Soon the two other caches were located. They contained guns, ammunition, traps, Indian goods, beads and gaudy cottons. New equipment from the caches was distributed among the excited trappers.

Robinson, Rezner and Hoback appropriated all

the beaver traps and held a private conference. Presently they came to Stuart in a group.

"You see, we've been figgerin' it out," began Robinson with some embarrassment, "as how our goin' back to the settlements is goin' to be mighty hard on these here chilluns. We've hardly got clothes on our backs and they'd put us to work behind a plow. They'd make farmers out of us." He paused and added, "And a trapper can't sink no lower. It just ain't accordin' to nature."

"Besides, I reckon the beaver would miss us. They'd just pine away," said Hoback, thoughtfully scratching his ear.

"An' the white b'ars would git no exercise treein' hunters," put in Rezner earnestly.

"Scalp my old head, this coyote just can't leave the mountains. Trappin's in the blood," continued Robinson desperately. And then more calmly, "Maybe you could let us have a few traps and some ammunition, maybe enough fer, say, a two-year hunt."

"I'm mighty sorry that you want to leave us," replied Stuart. "We're about to go through hostile Indian country and need every man and you three are of the best. Besides, I should think you had had enough of starvation and misery to last you a couple of years. It's no time for brave men to desert."

Then he was silent, looking at the three gaunt and forlorn trappers. As they stood there against the wild landscape of canyon and mountain they seemed to blend with their strange world, to be an inseparable part of the fantastic life of the Far West. Though a very young man, Stuart was a wise judge of human nature. A half-remembered saying ran through his mind—something about "there will his heart be also." That was it. "Where a man's treasure is there will his heart be also."

"However," he continued, "there's no use asking a man to do something when his heart is not in it. The American Fur Company is looking for beaver pelts, and be sure you trade in your catch to Mr. Hunt at Astoria. Take the traps and enough ammunition. For the rest of your fixin's you had better wait for the arrival of John Reed's party here in a few days. They are coming here to lift the caches and will be disappointed when they don't find them. You will pay Mr. Hunt in beaver skins for the supplies I have advanced you."

The trappers were delighted with this generous treatment. However, Mr. Miller, their companion, was glad to part with them as he had enough of the wilderness and was longing for civilization. He was an intelligent and trained observer and so was to serve as guide to the Stuart party eastward across the Rockies.

Visitors

(September 1, 1812)

The seven travelers loaded their pack horses with their new equipment, tightened the girths on their horses and rode off, waving farewell to the three shaggy mountain men and to Caldron Linn.

Mr. Miller persuaded them to leave the northwest course of the Snake and bear southeast through a barren landscape burnt brown and lifeless by the fierce summer sun. For several days they followed the Bear River where the Wasatch Range rose to the west. As they advanced up this stream they procured a lean diet by fishing.

The sun was sinking behind the mountains as they sat eating their evening catch of fish. Glancing up, Stuart said suddenly, "Indians." From nowhere a half dozen savages had appeared.

"They look like Crows," said McLellan, reaching for his rifle.

A huge Indian came forward. He was over six feet tall, his half-naked body superbly muscled. His long black hair hung loosely to his waist. His brutal face gleamed with malice and under his low brows shone eyes like a wolf's.

As this savage and Crooks palavered in the Indian sign language, more Indians kept appearing until a band of twenty warriors surrounded the camp. The chief was apparently friendly and eager to trade on the morrow. The Indians returned to their camp and the white men spent a watchful night with their rifles ready.

Next morning Stuart bartered in a fine supply of buffalo meat. In return the Indians wanted ammunition. But the white men refused, not wanting to contribute to their own murder. As the trappers broke camp and mounted their horses the tall chief came up to Stuart and in a rage threatened to haul him out of his saddle. Stuart coolly pressed his pistol against the Indian's head and the rest of his party leveled their guns at the other savages. The Indians vanished into the underbrush and the huge chief, suddenly changing his expression, began to laugh. He yelled and howled and shook with mirth. Stuart was unaccustomed to seeing an Indian laugh but he smiled grimly and the party rode off, leaving a present of twenty rounds of powder with the chief.

Horse Thieves

Miller led them eastward across a valley where the mountains rose on all sides, eternal and immense. High up on a peak ahead a thin black column of smoke rose like a pencil mark to the sky. Presently another answered across the valley, and a column could be seen through the clear air far to the south. The travelers looked grimly at each other, knowing only too well what the signals meant. Soon there would be hundreds of Indians on their trail from any or all directions. The Indian signals made them uncertain and confused. Did Miller know where he was leading them? If they turned north they would surely cross Hunt's route of the year before. That was the way they knew.

"We've got to go east," said Miller angrily. "It's where the sun rises—there across the valley—any fool can see that. Keep east and sooner or later you must cut across the north-south ranges of the Continental Divide. I figure that a hundred miles eastward across the valley we will cross the Wind River mountains into the plains."

The travelers looked uneasily at the smoke columns. "We will look for Hunt's route. It's the way we came. That's the way we are sure of."

"All right," said Miller. "It's your responsibility. From now on you take over. I'll go along."

For a week they rode north through mountain country that grew ever more difficult. No Indians appeared, but they did not know who might be slinking in the ravines and gullies or watching from the other side of the ridge. At night they kept watch with the uneasy feeling that hostile presences lurked everywhere unseen.

When they reached the Snake they camped for several days, rested the fagged horses and felt secure. They were out of the hostile Crow country.

The men were breakfasting leisurely and the horses grazed a short distance away. Suddenly an Indian yell broke out and a savage horseman charged through the herd of horses waving a red blanket. After him came a howling band of savages stampeding the herd before them. From the opposite direction another band dashed in for the travelers' baggage. These the surprised trappers managed to head off. Within a few minutes the whole demoniac band, yelling and laughing, had disappeared with every last one of the horses.

East Is West

In the trappers' vocabulary there was no word for "lost." A self-respecting mountain man had no use for it. But a great hunter (Daniel Boone) admitted that at one time he had been "right bewildered" for three days.

For some days Mr. Stuart's party had secretly suspected that they were "right bewildered."

Added to this was the absolutely "gone" feeling of being without horses some thousand wilderness miles from nowhere in particular. The prospect of being scalped, frozen or starved in the wilderness was remotely unpleasant, but being without a horse produced a feeling in the pit of the stomach that was indescribable. Gloomy silence settled on the camp. It was several hours before anyone spoke. Then their spirits roused in a rebound of energy, hope and zest for adventure. After all, it was all in a trapper's day's work.

"Let's get goin', men," called Stuart. "Sort out the junk. Pack what you need and throw the rest in the river. Guess we'll be traveling shank's mare till we can pick up a few Indian ponies."

For two days they trudged over rough country, bending under their heavy packs and fixins. Deciding to cross to the north side of the river, they built two stout rafts and embarked. The rafts floated surprisingly well in the swift current that carried them rapidly downstream, four men on one and three on the other.

This proved to be such an agreeable form of travel that it was decided to continue downstream on the rafts till they were clear of the mountain range which towered above them. At night the voyageurs pulled the rafts up on the bank and camped. They caught beaver in an old trap someone had kept from the cache, and as game became plentiful they again lived well.

Mr. Miller had become resigned to this progress.

He sat cross-legged on the raft and pulled at an old pipe stuffed with aromatic cuttings from his skin tobacco pouch which had long since been emptied. Occasionally he made sarcastic comments half to himself.

"I suppose you will be pulling into St. Louis any day now. Tying up right at the door of the Rocky Mountain House, no doubt," he said pleasantly. "This will be surprising, though, considering that we are traveling west at five miles an hour straight toward where we came from."

Then after a while he said, "Any cross-eyed daffy beaver pup can see that the sun rises in the east, but we are far smarter than that. We are traveling *west* toward the sunrise. We're going to prove that east is west, you might say."

No one paid any attention to Mr. Miller. His opinions had long since been discredited. The expedition was living the life of Riley, and though not quite sure of where they were going, they were getting there fast and easily. The river had wound in so many directions it was hard to tell for long which way they were going.

Eastward Across the Divide
(October 8-21, 1812)

After a week's river travel the mountain range leveled out. They had not found Hunt's trail and so again they shouldered their packs and, leaving the river, plunged northward into the wilderness.

The party was now entering the country of the Blackfeet. Day and night they were haunted by fear of the dread presence of these terrors of the wilderness. They dared not fire a gun for fear of bringing these merciless killers upon them.

As they approached a steep mountain it was decided that it would be safer to climb over than go around it where, in the valleys, the Blackfeet might be hunting. Like young wildcats they sprang up the rocky slopes. All but McLellan. He was not young and his feet were desperately sore and dragged wearily under his heavy pack. In rage and despair he threw away his pack and yelled that he would climb no farther but would take his chance with the Blackfeet and go down the valley and around the mountain.

"Come back, Mac, you fool! Come back!" his companions shouted. But he only turned, shook his fist and disappeared into the wooded bottom land.

From the snowy summit they looked across a valley at the three peaks of the Tetons—the Pilot Knobs, as Hunt had called them. They could now see the lay of the land and at last get some sense of direction. In the valley below they watched a moving speck.

"It's McLellan. He's ahead of us," shouted Crooks to the others.

At their camp in the valley they bagged five elk and feasted. For some days Crooks had been ailing and was stricken down with fever. The journey was now a race against winter and starvation. A terrible decision had to be made about Crooks.

"It's his life or ours. We must leave him and go on," said the men to Stuart.

"No you don't," said Stuart firmly. "We're going to stick together. He will be fit again in a few days. While I'm alive we will stay here with him."

They gave Crooks an Indian sweat bath and in four days he staggered to his feet. The six men again started on.

They clambered up through the Teton pass and, shivering with the cold, descended along the rim of dizzy precipices. They were now at the head of the Green River Valley.

To the east the travelers saw the Wind River mountains, the great wall of the Continental Divide, the backbone of the continent. The party would follow this southeastward until they found a passage through the mountains to the great plains. In the valley they hoped to find plenty of buffalo but came only upon skulls and bones in the wake of some Indian hunting party that had driven off the great herds.

For three days they staggered on without food. In the dry grass they came upon the emaciated body of a man. It was McLellan. He was still alive but was too weak to lift his head.

He wanted them to leave him alone to die where he was, but the men hauled him to his feet, cheered him up and helped him to stumble forward. Far ahead they sighted a dark object. It was a lone buffalo, an ancient bull, the last of the herd. The hunters crept up on their hands and knees till they were in range and all fired together.

"He must have been with ole man Noah in the Ark," said Crooks, as the men fell upon the carcass with their knives, tearing with their teeth at pieces of raw meat. Stuart persuaded them to make a meat soup and drink this first. All through the night the men bolted the tough meat, slept, waked and bolted again.

With full stomachs, life, strength, courage came back and they moved out on the trail again with a steady stride that ate up the long miles. Farther down the level valley they crossed the broad trace that had been an Indian highway down the valley for centuries. Suddenly the travelers came upon a large encampment of Shoshones.

These Indians were nearly as poor and miserable as themselves, for they had been robbed not long before by a powerful band of Crows. Together the two parties sat and smoked the pipe of peace, cursed the Crows and bartered for what each valued most. Stuart's party procured buffalo meat and, best of all, a venerable horse. He was sag-backed and bony, but to the trappers who packed their baggage on his back he was the most beautiful horse in the world.

The seven companions now marched on toward the Wind River mountains following an Indian trail until this turned off toward the northeast.

Bearing ever southeastward, they crossed the desert land that lay south of the Sweetwater Moun-tains. Finding a gap through the mountains, they came out on the banks of the Sweetwater River as it wound out of the mountains toward the vast slopes of the eastern plains. They were out of the Rockies at last.

Winter Quarters

Years later Ramsay Crooks wrote that they had come through the South Pass on October 21 and so were the discoverers of the historic gateway to the Far West through which the Oregon immigrant trains and the Gold Rush poured in after years. Certainly they came very near it and the writers of history still argue the question.

Slowly they made their way eastward, passing through the fantastic gateway called "the Devil's Gate" and by the lonely mound of "Independence Rock." Threading a deep canyon, they came out on a rocky ledge and looked down into a chasm where the river leaped furiously over precipices of red rock. "The Fiery Narrows" was the name the trappers gave to the Canyon of the Upper Platte.

These were the first white men to gaze on this vast and majestic landscape. But they were not looking for scenic beauty. They must master the stern menace of its distances or succumb to its grim and cruel indifference.

It was the last of October and a northeast wind that chilled them to the bones was blowing coldly across the uplands. Winter was close at hand. Some urged that they find a sheltered spot and "hole up" for the winter.

"But," said Miller, "we are going down toward the plains where it will be warmer. With good weather and easy going across the prairies we can make the Missouri in six weeks. By New Year's we will be in St. Louis. Let's keep going."

Again Miller was voted down.

The weather worsened, the rain turned to sleet, a northeaster blew through their tattered and blackened elk-skin shirts. Farther on they came to a bend in the river where the cottonwood trees grew tall. Everywhere there was buffalo sign. This was the perfect spot for winter quarters. Miller was plumb locoed. His companions were unanimous in their decision to winter here.

Fat of the Land
(November 1 — December 13, 1812)

Four or five hunters left camp seeking for game. Within two or three days they had shot forty-seven fat buffalo. It looked like a good winter. In a couple of days they had constructed a snug log cabin with six-foot walls eight by eighteen feet. All they needed was deer skin for warmer clothes. The hunting party went off into the mountains and bagged twenty-eight big-horn and black-tailed deer.

The cabin bulged with smoked meat. Buffalo tongues and other choice parts hung from the ceiling. Hump ribs of fat cow, marrow bones, and other delicacies were the daily menu. Flesh came back to the men's lean bones. Their cheeks grew fat and they wiped their greasy beards on their new deerskin shirts and grinned. Even Mr. Miller was amiable, and McLellan became good-natured.

Songs and tall tales regaled the evenings around the fire in the fragrant cabin while the wind howled and moaned outside.

One day at break of dawn, while the cabin shook with thunderous snores, there burst suddenly from the woods the yelping Indian war cry. Stuart jumped up, crept to the door and looked out. In the gray light he could see a score of Indians in full war paint. In a moment the cabin was roused and the men were reaching for their rifles.

"Break out the clay between the logs and give 'em hot lead," urged McLellan.

"They are the same Arapahoes that robbed me a year ago," said Miller.

"No," Stuart ordered firmly, "let's try a peace parley first." He and a companion stepped out of the door. Making the peace sign, Stuart crossed to the woods and took the painted chieftain by the hand.

The chief explained that they were a band of twenty-three Arapaho braves on the warpath in pursuit of a party of Crows who had attacked and robbed their village. They had been on the trail for almost sixteen days without food. They had been terribly hungry for a long time.

"We can take care of that," said Stuart, ushering the chief and several warriors into the cabin. "Help yourself," pointing to the heaps of dried meat.

The Indians ate almost continuously for twenty-four hours. Large helpings were passed outside to the rest of the party. For two solid days they gorged without stopping. Then, somewhat appeased, the savages said they must be going but would take what they could carry of the white man's good meat.

"When we have beaten the Crows we will return and give you horses for your journey, but you must now give us ammunition to destroy the Crows," said the chief good-naturedly.

"When you return with the horses we will give you the ammunition," replied Stuart.

Abruptly the Arapahoes filed off into the hills. "We can be thankful we still have our scalps even if most of the meat is gone," said Stuart wistfully.

"And we better make tracks for the Missouri pronto, before the red varmints come back. Next time there will be both the Arapahoes and the Crows," added Crooks.

The party again loaded the old horse with buffalo jerky and floundered off into the snowy landscape. For two weeks they worked their frozen way down the Platte in the bitter winter of the open plains. There was now not a tree in sight. Without wood and fire they would surely perish in this frozen world.

There was nothing for it but to turn back and drag their way back till they found timber. It was seventy-five terrible miles before the party came upon a growth of cottonwoods. Again the men framed a cabin and hunted buffalo which they found in abundance. Six bleak weeks passed. With March the cold receded. The sun grew warm. The men hewed two canoes out of cottonwood logs, loaded them with food and fixins and set off. The river was a gleaming expanse of water nearly a mile wide. To their disgust they could not find a channel deep enough to float the canoe. "A mile wide and one inch deep," was the way travelers described the Platte.

The party loaded their skeleton horse and again plodded on through mild days and cold nights. The prairie stretched empty to the horizon. They marched on. It seemed they had been slogging across the level emptiness for centuries. Perhaps there were no more people in the world. Perhaps they would keep marching on in a grotesque procession through empty space forever.

Then the prairie began to come alive. The green grass was thrusting up. Suddenly with a wild honking, thousands of geese and ducks rose in the air and the sky was filled with beating wings. The men came upon deserted Indian villages surrounded by piles of buffalo skulls. In a ragged tent sat three ancient squaws. They seemed unbelievably old and spoke no word.

At last a moving speck showed in the distance. A man. The travelers soon caught up with him, an Indian who led them to his Oto village. Here they found two white men, the first they had met in months. The trappers were very near the Missouri.

The Otos built them a twenty-foot bull boat for descending the river. From the two traders they learned that the world was still inhabited by white men and as usual was at war. This time the battle was between Great Britain and the United States. The redcoats had burned Washington. The trappers looked at each other, guessing what this might mean for Astoria.

Journey's End
(April 30, 1813)

Hospitable St. Louis delighted in celebrating departures and arrivals from the Far West. The appearance of the seven wanderers from Astoria was a dramatic surprise that occasioned a special celebration. After the tragic news of the *Tonquin* disaster, Astoria had been written off as lost in the minds of most Missourians. This sudden arrival with news of the success of the Hunt party was a tremendous victory, and St. Louis was well aware of all it might mean for the future prosperity of the Republic.

There were plenty of men in St. Louis who knew what it took to cross the Rockies. General William Clark, Superintendent of Indian Affairs, was one of them for he had done it twice himself. The travelers were welcomed into the frontier town as nothing less than heroes.

Seven men had come across three thousand miles of unmapped wilderness, partly by ways no white man had ever trod before, through tribes of hostile savages. They had endured starvation and unspeakable sufferings. Not a man had been injured or lost (excepting for the mental illness of John Day at the start). It had not been necessary to kill a single Indian. This was a masterpiece of wilderness skill and tactics, as well as of courage and endurance. It was true that there had been mistakes and blunders but all obstacles had been surmounted.

William Hunt and gallant young Robert Stuart had opened up the highway of American destiny across the continent to the Pacific. It was to become famous in after years as the Oregon Trail.

Mr. Astor sat moodily by the window as the late dusk of the spring evening fell over Manhattan. He had had no news in the months since his expedition had left St. Louis. As usual the butler appeared and handed him the evening papers. He fumbled anxiously among them for a moment and then tore open the Missouri *Gazette*. What he read on the first page sent a warm glow through him. It was the account of Stuart's and Crooks' arrival in St. Louis with the news of Astoria.

In June came the long-expected letter from Robert Stuart, dated St. Louis, May 1. It confirmed the good news and gave details of the success of Mr. Hunt and the settlement of Astoria. The supply ship *Beaver* had arrived safely at the Columbia. The United States Government was to send the frigate *Adams* to defend the post at Astoria.

Mr. Astor was not given to emotional lapses but of this moment he said, "I felt ready to fall upon my knees in a transport of gratitude."

PART
IV
THE DREAM
FADES

Farewell Astoria
(August 4, 1812)

As the *Beaver* rounded Cape Disappointment on her northern course, Mr. Hunt stood at the rail gazing at the diminishing fort with a melancholy premonition. The ship was on her way to the Russian post at New Archangel, Alaska, where Mr. Hunt, as Astor's representative, was to treat with the Russian Commandant on company matters. Hunt planned to be back at Astoria by October.

In the meantime the command at Astoria fell upon Mr. Duncan McDougal. Though himself a British subject, McDougal must now defend Mr. Astor's settlement from the British, the Northwesters, and the Indians as well as hunger and whatever disasters the dark forests and the foreboding future might bring.

He did not have to wait long for news that boded no good to Astoria. On January 16, gloomy and bedraggled, Donald McKenzie arrived at the fort. He had cached his furs and abandoned his post in the back country to bring back startling news.

A party of Northwesters under two men named MacTavish and LaRoche had informed him that Britain and the United States were now at war. MacTavish had said that the British man-of-war *Isaac Todd* would arrive at the Columbia in March to take possession of Astoria.

"The British Navy is comin' to destroy us," said McKenzie.

"Then we'll be gittin' no more supplies from the States," said McDougal.

"The Injuns won't trade with us," said McKenzie.

"Have ye any more encouragin' news, mon?" asked McDougal.

"We must give up the business and leave the country," said McKenzie.

"The sooner the better," agreed McDougal.

The two partners shook hands and began to make arrangements.

McKenzie now returned up the Columbia to inform Clark and David Stuart of the decision to abandon Astoria. On the way he met MacTavish and his party, who were gaily on their way down the river to meet the *Isaac Todd* and join in the capture of Astoria.

Clark, Stuart, and McKenzie met at the rendezvous on the Walla Walla and returned with their furs to Astoria, reaching there on June 14, 1813. They found McDougal busily and hopefully preparing to evacuate the fort by July 1.

The four partners held a grand council. Clark and Stuart bitterly opposed surrender, saying that the fur catch had been plentiful and that their prosperity had just begun. McKenzie and McDougal argued that no supply ships had arrived, that the British warship would soon appear, and that their fur business had been a failure; they could not compete with the Northwesters.

McKenzie's gloomy councils had their effect. On July 1, 1813, the four partners signed a long list of cowardly arguments for surrender and announced their intention to abandon Astoria on June 1st of the following year. The clerks and young Americans who wanted to defend the fort had no vote.

Meanwhile the arrogant MacTavish and his jaunty crew had arrived at Astoria and planted the British flag under the very walls of the fort. MacTavish very happily agreed to send the manifesto of surrender back to Mr. Astor for the partners.

For this expedition Mr. McDougal furnished the provisions from the fort.

On August 20, 1813, the ship *Albatross* arrived at Astoria, bringing, at last, the long missing Hunt. After a year's fruitless wandering in the Pacific he had arrived too late to save Astoria. Heartsick at the betrayal of Astoria, Hunt sailed away within a week to seek a ship in which to remove Mr. Astor's property including a fortune in beaver, which was left meanwhile in McDougal's charge.

On October 7th a new detachment, called the Northwest Brigade, arrived with powers to purchase the fort and its belongings. The men of the brigade ran up the British colors under the walls of the fort.

Inside, the angry Americans started to haul up the Stars and Stripes, but McDougal forbade it, although in case of trouble the Britishers were almost without ammunition and provisions. The sixty men in the fort were well supplied and believed they could have easily destroyed the enemy camped under their guns. It was with rage and disgust that the Americans learned that McDougal was furnishing the Northwest Brigade with supplies from the fort's provisions. Worse still, he agreed to sell to the Northwesters the furs which he was instructed to keep until Hunt could remove them. He accepted the offer of $40,000 for furs valued at $100,000.

The Canadian trappers swaggered about the fort, bragging that they had outsmarted, out-traded, and out-maneuvered their rivals. Inside the fort the enraged Americans cursed McDougal and McKenzie as traitors and rogues, but as they were only a small minority they could do nothing about the situation.

McDougal, happy that everything was working according to plan, watched the horizon for the expected arrival of the British warship *Isaac Todd*. On November 30th a ship appeared off Cape Disappointment and anchored in Baker's Bay. McDougal rowed out to greet the stranger. He was ready to declare his nationality as either British or American, depending on what flag the ship carried.

He was relieved to find that the ship was the British frigate *Racoon*, under the command of a Captain Black. This officer was prepared to destroy the fort and was expecting to secure a large amount of loot. He was bitterly disappointed to find that the fur treasure of the little fort had been carried off by his fellow countrymen of the Northwest Company.

When McDougal returned to the fort he found his father-in-law, Comcomly, the old one-eyed chief of the Chinooks, waiting with his braves in full war paint. The Indians had seen the "war canoe" and, seizing their weapons, had come to defend Astoria against the British. When the Indians learned that McDougal had surrendered the fort to the British, they turned scornfully away.

As Comcomly left, he said contemptuously, "I thought my daughter had married a great brave. Now I see she has married a squaw."

As a matter of routine the disappointed Captain Black formally took possession of Astoria and the country around it in the name of his Britannic Majesty King George IV. He ran up the Union Jack, rechristened the post "Fort George," and on December 31, 1813, sailed away.

On February 20, 1814, eighteen months after his departure, Hunt returned to Astoria in the ship *Pedlar*. He found that Mr. Astor's property had been sold to the British by the accommodating McDougal.

When Hunt demanded Mr. Astor's furs, McDougal replied that he would gladly sell them to him at a figure fifty per cent over and above the purchase price paid by "his company." Hunt learned, to his amazement, that McDougal had been for some time a partner in the Northwest Company.

Mr. Hunt "expressed his indignation in the strongest terms," wrote Washington Irving, putting it very mildly. At Hunt's insistence McDougal surrendered the papers of the Pacific Fur Company (which he had carefully copied for his new partners). He also delivered to Hunt the Northwest Company's draft in Mr. Astor's favor in payment for the furs. With these Hunt boarded the *Pedlar* on April 3rd, and her sails soon faded out on the gray horizon.

Silently the white Pacific fog crept in, veiling the abandoned fort and shrouding the ancient forests that had watched the slow centuries pass and waited for Man the changer, the destroyer, the builder.

Dorion's Squaw
(April 4, 1814)

A brigade of the Northwest Company going up the Columbia from Astoria was passing the mouth of the Walla Walla. With them were the last of the Astorians. A child's voice called from the shore, *"Arretez donc! Arretez donc!"* . . . "Stop! Stop!"

When the men went ashore they found Dorion's squaw and her two children. She had a story she wanted to tell them for remembrance, a last chapter in the saga of Astoria:

Dorion and his family had gone up the Snake River with a large trapping party under John Reed for the winter hunt. Later they were joined by the three inseparables—Hoback, Robinson and Rezner. The brigade had established winter quarters on the Boise River and small bands of trappers had gone up the beaver streams, setting their traps.

With the trappers, Rezner and LeClerc, Dorion had followed a beaver stream for five days, taking many pelts. His squaw and the two children kept the camp, cooked the meals, and dressed the furs.

After the day's work she had prepared the evening meal as usual and was expecting the return of the hunters.

The firelight flickered on the Indian woman's impassive face. The broiling meat filled the air with a fragrant aroma. The hungry children watched the cooking meat.

Suddenly the woman heard someone stumbling through the brush. In a moment LeClerc staggered into camp. Blood was flowing down his white face. He was desperately wounded.

"The Nez Percé!" he groaned. "They jumped us over the traps. Dorion and Rezner are killed!" Then he sank heavily on the ground.

The Indian woman moved quickly. Deftly she bound up LeClerc's wounds. Then, snatching the meat and some dried salmon, she rolled them in a buffalo robe. In a few minutes she had rounded up two horses. She helped the wounded man onto one and mounted herself and the children with the food and skins on the other. They rode off into the darkness. It was a five days' journey to Reed's cabin but she was sure of the way.

On the third day they saw dark spots moving on the snow. A file of Indian horsemen was crossing the valley. Dismounting, the squaw and her party hid in the brush until it was safe to go on. They built no fire that night. Dorion's squaw hugged her two children under the buffalo robe against the January cold. In the morning LeClerc was dead.

Late that day Dorion's squaw reached the cabin. It was empty and looted. There were fresh blood-stains everywhere and signs of a terrible struggle. For two days Dorion's squaw rode on toward the Blue Mountains. The food was nearly gone and she knew she could not cross the mountains in winter. The second night she found a sheltered spot with wood and a spring of water. The children helped set up a tent of beaver skins on the willow poles their mother had cut.

Skillfully the Indian woman made fire with Le-Clerc's flints, and with his knife she cut the horses' throats. For days she and the children smoked the meat that would keep them alive through the long winter weeks.

By mid-March the food was nearly gone. The Indian woman packed what she and the children could carry on their backs and thus the three started on foot across the mountains. With primi-tive instinct, wilderness craft, and the guiding of the Great Manitou, they came out on the Walla Walla River and down its banks to the Columbia. There Dorion's squaw found the Walla Walla Indians. They gave her hospitable welcome, for they knew courage when they met it.

No one took the trouble to record her name, but she is remembered for her loyalty and fortitude and she lives in the long memory of the West as, simply, "Dorion's Squaw."

Promise

Mr. Astor's plan was a great vision of expanding American enterprise that included all North America. It was magnificently conceived and practically planned.

But in the arduous tasks of carrying it through, unforeseen circumstances were stacked against it, time and distance, war, treachery, national loyalties, and slow minds.

It would be three decades before the call to Oregon would bring Americans in the white top wagon trains by the thousands across the Oregon Trail that Hunt's starving voyageurs had traveled so perilously.

The promise of Astoria had not been lost, only postponed. The Astorians' epic march across the continent had shown the way for free enterprise to open up the wealth and power of a new world for a great nation and people. In less than a hundred years the pioneers and statebuilders would come in steamboat, covered wagon and iron horse to raise up seas of wheat and corn, to reap the wealth of the mountains and plains and to build the great free cities of the nation forever united from sea to sea.

Epilogue
1814-195-

The Trail Breakers

We remember, we do not forget, oh Trail Breakers searching
The river courses to their secret sources
Platte, Yellowstone, Sweetwater, Columbia
Seeking out the passes over the Shining mountains across
The Big Horns, Bitterroot, Medicine Bow,
The Tetons, the Cascades, the Sierras.
The wind in the Great South Pass remembers the lost trappers.

Under the red bluffs the wagon trains pass, the prairie schooners
The white tops in dusty processions along the Oregon Trail, the Santa Fe
Bringing the Prairie Breakers, the plowmen, the bull-tongued plows
To cut the tough sod in Nebraska, in the Dakotas.
Armies of green corn for Iowa, for Minnesota the golden sea of wheat
Pioneer mothers listening to the wolf song in the twilight
In the sod huts of the Kansas prairie. . . .

Mule train, stage coach, pony express pushing
  through the mountain passes
The Iron Horse rolls spouting black clouds and
  cinders
The Continental Express roars on, faster, faster,
  faster.
On the six-lane highways the sleek speeders are
  streaking west
The Airliner drones across the sky, nine hours to
  California.
The Jet Plane, the Supersonic Rocket, the mush-
  room blast of the Atomic Age!

Astoria, the log fort forgotten between the forest
  and the sea
Lost in the white sea fog and the drip of the per-
  petual forest.
For the time is not ripe for the dream, a hound
  rushing ahead
Of slow destinies, for Astor's encompassing dream.
The vision is true but the hour has not come, only
  the voice
Calling in the wilderness, "The vision is yet for an
  appointed time
But in the end it shall speak, and not lie;
Though it tarry, wait for it, because it will surely
  come,
It will not tarry."

Index

178

180

LANDMARK BOOKS

★